Mindful Paths: Steps Towards A Living Spirituality
By Constance McClain and James Anthony Walker
Published 2018 by Your Book Angel
Copyright © Rev. Constance McClain and Rev. James Anthony Walker

To order this title please contact: inquiries@mindfulpaths.com

Printed in the United States

Edited by Keidi Keating

Layout by Christi Koehl

ISBN: 978-1-7320268-8-9

MINDFUL PATHS

Steps towards a living spirituality

REV. CONSTANCE MCCLAIN
REV. JAMES ANTHONY WALKER

Endorsements

Mindful Paths: Steps Towards A Living Spirituality by Constance McClain and James Anthony Walker provides an inspiring compendium of spiritual wisdom and practice along with practical worksheets to help each reader define and refine the depth and breadth of their own spiritual being. Based on decades of study with many great teachers, and in turn teaching hundreds of their own students, I highly recommend it both for beginners and those who have already set out on their spiritual journey.

-Ed Bastian, PhD
Founder, Spiritual Paths Institute
Author, "*Living Fully, Dying Well: Reflecting on Death to Find Your Life's Meaning*"

Even though you really don't know where you are going, sometimes you need a roadmap to get there. Revs. Constance McClain and James Anthony Walker's Mindful Paths: Steps Towards A Living Spirituality is that roadmap.

It doesn't presume to know who you are or where you need to go, but invites you to discover both through deep and practical exercises of self inquiry. This book requires both light reading and heavy lifting. Read the book. Do the work.

-Rabbi Rami Shapiro
Author, "*The Sacred Art of Lovingkindness*"

This new collaboration between Revs. Constance McClain and James Anthony Walker is a gem of a book, and a revelation. With great care and ease, they offer a loving introduction to spirituality as a vital dimension to our health and well-being which is deeply compelling — and potentially life-changing.

As method, they only ask for our honest, personal investment in ourselves — and therefore to the means affording a more spiritual life. They systematically ask us to consider the big questions of our deepest reality, and invite us to become increasingly aware of the rich inner life uniquely our own.

Whether you are currently engaged in a religious path, or instead find yourself to be "spiritual but not religious," their compassionate work is an opportunity to deepen and grow. Their work is user-friendly and extremely timely, for it encourages our consideration of the impact and transformation that spirituality can have an each of us as individuals — and therefore on our culture at large, sorely in need of our loving care and consciousness.

Highly recommended.

-Rev. David B. Wallace
Dean, One Spirit Interfaith Seminary, NYC

If you find that you are embarking on a personal journey of spirit, I encourage you to avail yourself of the warm and wise guidance of the Revs. Constance McClain and James Anthony Walker. Their own sacred journeys have not been direct or easy, but those rough patches have afforded them an insight and generosity of spirit that simply radiates from these lovingly written pages.

Surrender to the sensible guidance of these two Divine tour guides. You can trust that they will point you in the direction that is exactly right for you.

-Rev. Tony Martin, LCSW
Dean, One Spirit Interfaith Seminary

This book is a welcome addition to the literature on mindfulness. Anyone, of whatever faith, or of none, can benefit from the valuable information, spiritual wisdom, and practical, doable steps towards a more meaningful and spiritual life within this wonderful book.

The exercises and lessons will lead the reader to a richer, more meaningful life, as well as to increased serenity and peace of mind. I am happy to endorse it without reservations.

-Rabbi Richard Ettelson, Ph.D.
Licensed Clinical Psychologist and Pastoral Counselor

Mindful Paths: Steps Towards A Living Spirituality is an extensive presentation on spirituality as an important dimension of our health — broken down, explained and fully supported with the aid of detailed self-help exercises. I was impressed by the threads of knowledge presented here, the extent to which they are all woven together, and their impact on that which I thought I knew, but didn't."

-Julie Taguchi, MD
Sansum Clinic Ridley-Tree Oncology Center

"It is in the struggle that we learn to fly." *Mindful Paths: Steps Towards A Living Spirituality* is a wonderful guide to reflection, and a thoughtful workbook for cultivating reverence, through actively engaging our soul across all dimensions of this amazing journey Home.

-Camille Hamilton Adams Helminski
Author, *"Ninety Nine Names of the Beloved"*

WHAT STUDENTS ARE SAYING

"This is easily one of the best classes that I have ever taken. It was a challenge because it made me look at myself, how I look at others… and why."

-Sarah

"I don't know of anything else like this! Professor McClain asks questions and wants students' involvement. This is a class about *you*. How you can become something more, and make a difference."

-Jason

"Constance really offers ways for anyone to change their life, if they are willing to invest the time in themselves. The class has done that for me, and more. She and her partner James often have different perspectives on the same topic, so there is always something to think about. Highly recommended!"

-Sharon

"As a single mother of four, this coursework has given me a greater sense of balance in my life, which has allowed me to be far more effective at home and at work."

-Crystal

"When I began this program, I was coming out of a very difficult period of alcohol and drug abuse. It has helped me in so many ways. I will be forever grateful."

-Justin

"My spirit was dormant until I took this class. Now my spirit and soul are wide awake, and soaring. I am forever grateful."

-Letty

"The spiritual journey is a journey of the heart, and it has given me an inner peace. Self-seeking slips away and being there to assist others has become one of life's great joys. This work has been so rewarding."

-Bruce

DEDICATION

To all my teachers past and present, deceased and alive, I thank you for your patience with me in my struggles to understand this life. You have enriched this world for me immeasurably.

I trust you know who you are: Ed Bastian, Cynthia Bourgeault, Swami Atmarupananda, Rabbi Rami Shapiro, Kabir and Camille Helminski

Dad, Mom: for the seed that was held to give me life.

To all of my dogs, cats, and horses: my life was always filled with your honesty, comic relief, and integrity.

To friends too many to name, but these I must ... for you are all my heart and soul:

Barbara Clark, Matthew Edwards, Maureen Eliot, Marsha Kramark, Suzanne Berger, Kathy Henry, Raeann Koerner, Nancy Frederickson, Melissa Reparetti-Stepien, Janise Rennie, and Steve Thompson.

To all of my therapists, physicians and nurses at: Cottage Hospital, Cottage Rehabilitation Hospital and Sansum Clinic over the past five challenging years. You brought me back from death and gave me my smile back.

To my beloved fiancé Reverend James Anthony Walker: for all your courage, love, and care during this most challenging era of my existence. Your support has been, and is, priceless. *You are my angel, and I love you.*

I love you all, throughout the centuries... when I know we will meet again.

I'm one fortunate woman.

-Rev. Constance McClain

HOW TO USE THIS BOOK

A few practical tips for you.

There are many ways to mature into our spirituality, but after ten years of working with college students here in Southern California, I've designed *one* way that has helped hundreds of students as they have embarked upon their spiritual journeys.

The book you're holding in your hands right now has come to you on purpose. You've been intrigued about growing your spirituality and embodying your highest self. You've been thinking how chaotic the world seems to be now, and how you'd like to manifest a life filled with more happiness, confidence and love… and far less confusion, dissatisfaction, and suffering.

We will help you get there.

It will be a highly personal journey, one that will change and challenge you. These changes, small and large, will happen on the way, and may reflect your personal insights into yourself. For that reason, we recommend you either purchase or create a journal for yourself to archive your thoughts along the way as you find yourself on this Mindful Path of self-discovery and spiritual awakening.

You'll find support for your meditation practice online at **www.mindfulpaths.com /meditations**, which comes with an open invitation to connect with us as questions and challenges may arise for you.

Along the way, if you feel that you're experiencing a personal crisis that requires medical or consultative support, we've offered a list of resources at the end of the book.

As a matter of practice, the exercises and assignments offered in this book are equally valid within a class or an individual context. The only distinction is the manner in which the work is prepared on your end:

If you're in a class, please type your work, and submit it in person, or if taken in an online or hybridized setting… by uploading it, or completing it online.

If you're doing the work on your own, and outside of a class setting, how you manifest it is up to you, but know that if you wish to record your work directly in the book, space has been provided for you.

Jim and I are excited that you're here and look forward to walking together along this more mindful path, towards a greater understanding of the Divine gift that we have all been given.

With Love and care,
Constance

THE BUTTERFLY

A small child spent hours watching a butterfly struggling
to emerge from its cocoon.

It managed to make a small hole, but its body was too large to get through it.
After a long struggle, it appeared to be exhausted,
and remained absolutely still.

The little one decided to help the butterfly and, with a pair of scissors,
cut open the cocoon, freeing the butterfly from its struggle.

But the butterfly's body was very small and wrinkled,
and its wings were all crumpled.

The child continued to watch his new friend, hoping that at any moment,
the butterfly would open its wings and fly away.
But nothing happened.

In fact, the butterfly spent the rest of its brief life dragging around
its shrunken body and shriveled wings,
incapable of flight.

While acting only out of kindness, the child simply didn't know that the tight cocoon and the
struggle of the butterfly to squeeze out of it was Nature's way
of training the butterfly, and of strengthening its wings.

Sometimes, a little extra effort is exactly what prepares us
for the next obstacle we face in our lives.
These struggles are a part of our journey, and they prepare us for what awaits.

It is in the struggle that we learn to fly.

—author unknown

TABLE OF CONTENTS

PREFACE 1

CHAPTER 1 - THE MINDFUL PATH AHEAD 6

    A Transformative Journey 7

CHAPTER 2 - SPIRITUALITY AND WELLNESS 13

    Your Thoughts on Spirituality 14

    Spiritual Self-Assessment 15

    SMEEPOS - The Seven Dimensions of Health 16

CHAPTER 3 - THE SPIRITUAL LENS OF PERCEPTION ... 24

    Spiritual Awakening 25

    Religion and Spirituality - *differences and similarities* ... 26

    What is the Soul? 31

    Impermanence 36

    Our Internal Compass - honoring our inner voice ... 38

    Your Spiritual Biography 41

    Cultivating the Heart 47

    An Examination of Heart Consciousness 51

    Thoughts are Things 53

    Knowing Thyself 56

    Reflection and Discernment 65

    Your World View - *and how it shapes your personal values* ... 67

TABLE OF CONTENTS

CHAPTER 4 - DEEP TRUTHS AND ROLE MODELS 73

 Divine Paradoxes 74

 Exemplars 77

CHAPTER 5 - CREATING A SAFE PLACE 85

 Sacred Space 86

CHAPTER 6 - THE BUILDING BLOCKS OF SPIRITUAL LANGUAGE 91

 Your Spiritual Alphabet 92

 48-Hour Presence 108

CHAPTER 7 - CULTIVATING OUR PRESENCE IN THE WORLD 113

 The Grace of Gratitude 114

 Taking Things for Granted 115

 How Often Are We Really Here? 117

CHAPTER 8 - BALANCE, PRESENCE, AND CHANGE 121

 The Thought Continuum 122

 Generating Equanimity 124

 Impediments Along the Way 127

 Seasons of the Soul 129

CHAPTER 9 - MEDITATION 133

 What is it, and Why do it? 135

TABLE OF CONTENTS

Vipassana or Insight Meditation 137

Walking Mindfulness Meditation 138

Metta Meditation 140

Zazen Meditation 141

Transcendental Meditation (TM™) 143

Breathing 145

CHAPTER 10 - MINDFULNESS 148

Four Characteristics, One State of Mind 149

Mindfulness Foundations 152

Mindful Writing 155

Mindful Eating 160

CHAPTER 11 - COMPASSION 166

Compassionate Listening 168

Sound Meditation 170

Self-Compassion 172

Compassion for Others 173

Integrating our Shadow-Self 175

Cultivating Spirituality in Relationships 179

Learning How to Face Grief 185

TABLE OF CONTENTS

CHAPTER 12 - SOME OF OUR FAVORITE SPIRITUAL PRACTICES   191

    Random Acts of Kindness   193

    Lectio Divina - *reading as a contemplative practice*   195

    Seeing Spirit - *encountering the Divine through visualization*   202

    Haiku   203

    Mudra   206

    Mantra   210

    Mandala   214

    Chakra Opening for Healing   217

    Gratitude   224

    The Healing Power of Forgiveness   228

CHAPTER 13 - THE SUM TOTAL OF OUR EXISTENCE   233

    Addressing Karma   235

CHAPTER 14 - THE SCIENCE OF MEDITATION   238

    Self-Directed Neuroplasticity and Meditation   239

CHAPTER 15 - OUR SACRED ALIGNMENTS   247

    Honoring Gaia, our Mother Earth   249

    Getting to the Heart of the Matter   254

    Journal Assignment Index   258

    Index   259

PREFACE

It's an inside job.

Below is a favorite quote from one of our most Beloved teachers, Jon Kabat-Zinn, and it is a subtle reminder that can benefit us all:

"Wherever you go, there you are."

Spiritual exploration is a personal pursuit. One that you, if you've picked up or been given this book, are ready to take. We sincerely hope that you'll slowly, mindfully work your way through it, in order to learn more about who you are, how you came to be who you are, and how to transform those parts of yourself you think will improve your life now. Then you will be ready to embark upon a more mindful path as you more fully embrace the present, and look ahead with integrity to the future.

It is our deepest hope that in doing so, one of your most profound discoveries will be that:

"Compassion is the essence of all spiritual practice."
-The 14ᵗʰ Dalai Lama, Tenzin Gaytaso

It's scary out there.

We live in a time filled with chaos and uncertainty, worldwide. As a contemporary humanity, we have no corner on the market, but over the history of the planet many continue to seek stability during these unsettling times, by turning their attention toward time-tested tools that can help.

In the past, this often meant turning outward to one of hundreds of faith traditions worldwide, to find equanimity, community, confidence, and the courage to go forward in life. But since the 1960s, here in the United States and in many other countries, young people have begun to move away from the churches, faith traditions, and definitions of community which served their parents and grandparents. Because even though these time-tested institutions were no longer approachable or authentic enough for a younger generation living in a significantly transformed world, they still found themselves yearning for more understanding and inner guidance for their lives… still yearning to find and develop their "highest self," but without some of the trappings of their ancestors.

Their numbers became so large, and their statistics so overwhelmingly unavoidable, that they emerged as a new category of spiritual seekers that author Sven Erlandson coined the SBNR… an acronym where they could begin to self-identify as those who had chosen not to become involved with organized religion, but who instead were 'spiritual but not religious,' still wanting to develop approaches to better evolving into their higher spiritual selves.

Our needs are changing.

Time has shown this as something more than an overnight sensation that is here today and gone tomorrow. The Pew Research Center conducted a 2012 study on SBNRs, and their findings gave us new vision to both their size and scope.

The number of Americans who do not identify with any religion has increased from 15% in 2007, to 20% in 2012, and a follow-up study has shown that number continues to experience significant growth… to 27% in 2017.

The depth and breadth of these approaches to spiritual growth are both eye-opening and potentially life-changing, and in this book, we'll walk you through a number of spiritual practices that will help you open your heart and mind, while becoming far less judgmental in your everyday life. This book is about the self-discovery of you, and how to begin to look at your world through a more mindful, authentic lens… one that is truly yours, and one where we can begin to better recognize the importance of working together to create a better world for ourselves, our children, and for all sentient beings.

This outlook asks us to expand our perspective of life itself, and to look at it through a much more panoramic lens. A lens of inclusiveness and care, not only for our families, but for Mother Earth herself, and all the species that she wraps in her constant, loving and non-judgmental care.

Living from this perspective is an inside job, and so we'll begin by better understanding how we witness the world, determining whether or not we witness it through a lens of non-judgment, kindness and compassion… or in some other way that may not even be truly our own.

Why is this larger, more holistic frame of reference so natural for some, and so difficult for others?

Spiritual health is a thing.

Perhaps one of the root causes is a lack of reverence for life itself, lost for so many in an increasingly disposable culture. Perhaps a deadening of our willingness and ability to communicate in a world that operates at light speed, where change comes at a pace which often exceeds our ability to absorb it. And so, we become numb to it.

Let's face it. Being human means we'll be wounded and scarred. This pain can either be mental, emotional or both, often manifesting in physical symptoms that can disrupt our lives, and often either shut down our ability or our willingness to cope with it. We believe that over thousands and thousands of years, this has left a deep wound in our collective heart and soul.

These wounds cry out to us to be healed. But with an empathy that is compromised, it has become increasingly difficult to hold something, anything… reverentially.

And so, *have these centuries old wounds weakened our sensitivities toward the world at large?* Imagine if we all woke up one morning feeling the collective pain and suffering of humanity. Could we regain our empathy, and our reverence for humanity? *Is this our problem, or at least part of the problem?*

We've written this book because we hope it can help us, together, to become a part of the solution to a world seemingly at war with itself. That when we live our lives with moral integrity, we can become more aware, more conscious, and far more awake to our unique potential to support others.

Religious scholars Andrew Harvey and Matthew Fox call this inner pulse 'sacred activism.' We believe that once an individual awakens to the call of sacred activism, life begins to blossom with possibility… the birthing of our spiritual freedom.

Once we begin tapping into this, through our mindful decision to grow spiritually, we can begin to connect with the sacred, holy and Divine through experiences and pathways that will strengthen our relationship to a vastly greater, ineffable world of which we are inextricably a part.

This is work which, as with so many practices that deliver exceptional rewards, achieves its desired outcome with our consistent dedication. One day at a time. And in the process, we trigger a blossoming. Much like the lotus flower eventually, patiently blooms from the mud, so do we. There are no shortcuts, even if we would like it to be so.

The Choice is Ours.

Allowing ourselves to be the spiritual beings that we are means that we first come to understand our values. Do we refuse to accept greed, dishonesty, cruelty, violence, discrimination or any other mindsets that, through our ego-based self-centeredness only compromise the other sentient beings with which we share this Earth?

If so, then we have begun to seek the sacred in our life. A life filled with meaning and purpose. Our divinity, wherein we reach to our highest potential as human beings.

As French philosopher Pierre Teilhard de Chardin so famously wrote:

> *"We are not human beings having a spiritual experience, we are spiritual beings*
> *having a human experience."*

We are here, now, breathing freely as an expression of the lifeblood of everything in this universe to which we are connected. A unique, living embodiment of something much greater. Something endlessly creative. Something arguably nothing less than Divine.

As we open ourselves up, safely, to the unifying experiences of exploring a more contemplative life, we cross a sacred bridge, into a world where confidence in our right-mindedness blossoms like a field of spring flowers. Where we begin to walk along our most meaningful path with full vision to life's infinite possibilities.

Crossing this bridge is a mystical experience all of its own, where we discover that, one step at a time nothing is frightening or overwhelming. Where our self-limiting thoughts release into the ether, and our confidence in the Divine within us grows, grounded in a powerfully-rooted, often intoxicating love for humanity, and for the wonder in the world around us.

If you've found yourself with his book in your hands, make no mistake... *it is here because it was meant to be here.* You are being called to a higher purpose. One of the main ways we cultivate and nurture this calling is through contemplative practice. These practices guide us on to better ways of living a humane, authentically human experience.

It's our joy to meet you here.

CHAPTER 1
The Mindful Path Ahead

A TRANSFORMATIVE JOURNEY
Spiritual transformation as a change in our relationship to life.

> *"The ego is as you think of yourself. You in relation to all the commitments of your life, as you understand them. The self is the whole range of possibilities that you've never even thought of. And you're stuck with your past when you're stuck with the ego. Because if all you know about yourself is what you found out about yourself, well, that already happened. The self is a whole field of potentialities to come through."*
>
> -Joseph Campbell
> *The Hero's Journey: Joseph Campbell on His Life & Work*

Fundamentally, **spiritual transformation** is a desired change in ones **sacred or spiritual relationship to life**. Psychologically, human beings have an inner pulse that wants to understand its place in the world. We are better humans when we connect ourselves to something greater or wiser than we understand ourselves to be. We feel we are better served in our life if we find a sense of meaning and motivating purpose for ourselves.

In pursuit of that connection, we seek out answers to the big questions in our lives. *Who am I? Why am I here? Where am I going?* These seem at first blush almost unanswerable, but if we have a willingness to examine who we are in the moment, the answers can come easily... by looking within *to our mind, our body, and our spirit.*

Our mind represents the flow of information through our nervous system. This includes all the information we process, moment by moment.

Our body is the vessel that holds all of our dreams, our aspirations, our past, our present, and our hopes for the future... a manifest reflection of the state of all of the dimensions of our health, for better, or for worse.

Our spirit animates us (the body and mind). Spirit is often used metaphysically to refer to our consciousness. It comes from the Latin word "spiritus," meaning "breath."

Each one of us has our own evolution of life, and each one of us goes through tests which are unique and challenging.

But certain things are common.

And we do learn things from each other's experience.

On a spiritual journey, we all have the same destination.

- A.R. Rahman

A closely related word to remember here also comes from the Latin "inspirare," to breathe. So remember to breathe... or literally, to infuse into the mind a message colored by a Divine influence! *That* *is at the very heart of spiritual transformation, and it's only a breath away.*

Why is living an inspired life important? Because it is completely co-mingled with the endless creativity of the universe, of Spirit. Life in all of its dimensions is constantly creating something new of itself, expressing itself in new and exciting ways. For us to live a life outside of that flow seems somehow less than what it should be.

And yet, we often do. We become creatures of habit, because it is comfortable, easy. Life is working just fine for us, so as the old saying goes: *why upset the apple cart?*

What we lose in the process is our ability to hear the subtle voices inside us. Our ability to hear our inner guide, that which many would call our intuition... that rarely steers us wrong, if only we are willing and able to hear.

And that is where so many of the practices we'll be discussing and experiencing will serve you well. They are the key to your inner world, where you can establish your connection to a higher source. You may not know at the moment how to get there. That's okay... you are at the beginning of this journey of spiritual transformation *and that takes a lifetime.*

It begins with nothing more than your desire to unearth the parts of you that you want to create, re-create, or co-create... rooted in a personal belief that there is a more evolved, conscious, authentic human inside of you. A decision to expand your life and awaken to the best human being you can possibly become.

So let's begin to locate that inner pulse of yours, in search of that higher, lighter self... the one that arises from a Divine source, or energy, known by any name comfortable for you. Our favorite words to describe this higher (Divine) energy are: Great Spirit, God, Christ Consciousness, Buddha Mind, The Ground of Being, and Source.

This is not an overnight sensation. Transformation, as with life, does not happen overnight, but is rather a series of "mini-transformative experiences" to which we open ourselves over a completely undetermined (and undeterminable) amount of time.

What is the allure of spiritual transformation? Perhaps the gift at its core is the prospect of simply being.

Spiritual practices and tools are powerful, but only as much so as our ability and willingness to embrace them. That may start with first taking the high altitude view and asking the big questions. Here's a few to ask yourself, so that you can begin to gain clarity on who you really are, and who you really want to be. Jot a few notes down to journal your initial thoughts:

JOURNALING ASSIGNMENT 1.1

Do I want a better me?

_____

_____

_____

_____

Am I doing what I really want to do? Am I being who I really want to be?

_____

_____

_____

_____

Do I want to change? Why?

_____

_____

_____

_____

How do I relate to myself and to others?

_____
_____
_____
_____

Have I found my own truth, or am I living someone else's?

_____
_____
_____
_____

Is my head even clear enough to see who I am?

_____
_____
_____
_____

Now, reflect over the choices, behaviors and decisions you've made in life, the ones that have gotten you this far... **non-judgmentally**.

At the root of all of these, there has been a learned behavior, an attitude or a belief that has driven your choices. _All that we're asking of you here is to pick one with which to start_. For each, you'll go through a two-step process. You're welcome to take as many topics into discernment in this way as you wish.

Here's a few examples to help get you started:

"I hold prejudice against people who are not like me, and I want this to stop."
"I really don't listen to what others have to say. My opinion is the only one that matters."

JOURNALING ASSIGNMENT 1.2

Part 1

Choose a specific behavior, attitude or belief of yours that will benefit you and others if you decide to transform it, in order to reach toward a more highly-evolved version of yourself.

_____

_____

_____

_____

_____

_____

_____

_____

_____

Part 2

See (visualize) yourself as completely and honestly as possible prior to your transformation. How do you feel about yourself? How do others feel about you? Describe the quality of your relationship.

Next, describe how making this commitment to transformation has changed your feelings. About yourself, about others, and about the quality of your relationships. What has changed?

_____

_____

_____

_____

_____

_____

_____

_____

_____

CHAPTER 2
Spirituality and Wellness

YOUR THOUGHTS ON SPIRITUALITY
Assessing your current viewpoint

Take a few moments to inventory your current understanding of what Spirituality is or isn't. There are no right or wrong answers. In our ongoing work together, this will provide a baseline from which we can better assess the shifts in your Spiritual Health as you progress through this book. *Enjoy!*

Please indicate whether you agree (A) or disagree (D) with these statements:

1   Spirituality is an open-minded practice, encouraging personal growth .. A   D
2   Spirituality means showing loving kindness to all living things .... A   D
3   Spiritual practice is intended to help us release anger, or forgive .... A   D
4   Spirituality promotes the self as most important in our awareness .... A   D
5   Spirituality allows us to hold on to our shadow (dark) side   .... A   D
6   Spirituality helps us recognize the interconnectedness of all life .... A   D
7   Spirituality promotes human domination over all other life .... A   D
8   Spirituality is focused on being a better human being   .... A   D
9   Spirituality helps us focus on the future... A   D
10 Spirituality acknowledges that cruelty is a necessary part of life .... A   D
11 Spirituality is an exclusive lifestyle which rejects science and religion ... A   D
12 Spirituality is an awareness of something greater than we can know ..... A   D
13 Spirituality is inclusive in its acceptance of all religions & philosophies .... A   D
14 Spirituality is dogmatic (filled with rules).. A   D
15 Spirituality uses prayer and meditation to help us grow personally .... A   D
16 Spirituality replaces our need for a religious commitment..................... A   D
17 Spirituality helps us become more compassionate human beings .... A   D
18 Spirituality embraces suffering as a necessary condition of life .... A   D
19 Spirituality helps us manage the ineffable (unknown) in our lives .... A   D
20 Spirituality teaches us how to better be in service to our
     planet & each other .... A   D

SPIRITUAL HEALTH SELF-ASSESSMENT
An initial inventory of an essential dimension of health

Our health is one of our most treasured assets. Yet, when we think of our health, we usually don't even consider perhaps the most important dimension of it… our Spiritual health.

This dimension is broad and deep, and it demands our reflection and discernment on **six primary qualities**. The key to health in this dimension, as with so many others, rests with your ability to sustainably hold them in your awareness, and in balance.

They are:

You are conscious and aware that your **character development** is important.

You have a sense of **meaning and purpose** for your life.

You understand that **intention** provides direction in your life.

You have a sense of **awe and wonder** about your life.

You have a **respect and reverence** for all living things.

You understand your **core values** and live in alignment with them.

Answer the following questions as honestly as possible.

JOURNALING ASSIGNMENT 2.1

Look over your answers in **Your Thoughts on Spirituality**. *How accurately do they reflect your current state of spiritual well-being?*

_____

_____

_____

_____

_____

_____

_____

At this point in your life, why do you believe your life will benefit by improving your Spiritual well-being?

_____

_____

_____

_____

SMEEPOS
An acronym that asks us to focus on the rich dimensions of our well-being

SMEEPOS stands for these seven unique, yet highly-interrelated dimensions of health:

Spiritual
Mental
Emotional
Environmental
Physical
Occupational
Social

Health and wellness are two concepts that have gained significant prominence in the academic world since the 1990s when the term "wellness" was so well-defined by Dr. Kenneth Pelletier from Stanford University:

> *"Health is a life lived well and fully, a life involved with other people, and with self-exploration of the emotions, the mind, the body and the spirit."*
>
> -Dr. Kenneth R. Pelletier

For the past thirty years, Americans have been struggling with their health, to the point where Big Pharma have allocated increasingly larger budgets to research and development of new products that manage the **symptoms** of the similarly increasing numbers of sick people in our country.

Here's an excerpt from a recent (2012) Bloomberg Ranking, showing the top 10 of the world's healthiest countries. The U.S. ranked 33rd:

The World's Healthiest Countries

Rank	Country	Health Grade	Total Health Score	Health Risk Penalty
1	Singapore	89.45%	92.52%	3.07%
2	Italy	89.07	94.61	5.54
3	Australia	88.33	93.19	4.86
4	Switzerland	88.29	93.47	5.17
5	Japan	86.83	91.08	4.25
6	Israel	85.97	91.97	6.00
7	Spain	84.36	91.26	6.90
8	Netherlands	84.09	88.40	4.31
9	Sweden	83.90	89.37	5.47
10	Germany	83.58	88.81	5.23

Is this the most dangerous epidemic that we are confronting in the US? The treatment of **symptoms**, rather than the treatment of **wellness**?

In fact, yes. Our domestic health rankings fly in the face of the size of our health care expenditures. Although we are not unique in the fact that the Western world treats symptoms rather than encouraging wellness, we are not convincingly rooted in a panoramic, proactive approach to it.

We are not one-dimensional organisms, nor do we live in a one-dimensional world, which begs the question: what are the dimensions of the human spirit that need to be identified and brought into balance with each other? *How do they interact with each other in support of our most vibrant health and wellness?*

Author's Note:
"We work today with seven distinct dimensions in our work with both students and private clientele whose ages encompass a wide range. It is an evolution of an acronym which I created thirty years ago to help students better understand the breadth of dimensionality which defines a life that promotes, in a proactive way, health and wellness.

spirituality is meant to take us beyond our tribal identity, into a domain of awareness that is more universal.

- Deepak Chopra

Most of the textbooks of the day made reference to six dimensions of health, so the acronym was originally SMEEPS. About ten years later, a seventh dimension showed up which better encompasses all of our most critical dimensions of health and wellness, so SMEEPS morphed into SMEEPOS, or if you were Irish, O'SMEEPS!"

–CM

Let's take a look at each dimension of wellness now:

Spiritual Wellness

In our own research, this dimension most often takes the lead ahead of all other dimensional development, because our spiritual development increases both our capacity and our understanding of an expansive, deep array of our best humanity, including: *compassion (for self and others), humility, empathy, equanimity, patience, forgiveness, kindness, generosity, and the ability to let go of negative emotions and experiences as you learn how to forgive yourself and others.*

Our spiritual dimension includes our sense of awe and meaning (your life's purpose), as well as our recognition and acceptance that all of humanity is interconnected and interdependent.

As humans, we gain a vital sense of fulfillment in our lives when we have a sense of meaning and purpose for it. Without these two essential elements, we often let a deeper experience pass us by, in favor of merely breathing air and occupying space, leaving the best of us unknown to ourselves and others.

Spiritually healthy people have both an awareness and a belief in a power at work in the universe, which is greater than themselves… call it God, Source, Christ Consciousness, Allah, Jehovah, Yahweh, the Tao, the Buddha, and many, many other names.

Mental / Intellectual Wellness

This is our "thinking" dimension. It is here where you develop your attitudes, beliefs, and your world view… your perceptions about the world, and your place in it. This dimension also houses your critically paired ability to 1) think critically and from that, 2) make informed decisions.

The key to your success in bringing this dimension into balance is how you use this dimension to make healthy choices for yourself, and in supporting those of others. The behaviors which you reason through this dimension can bring either positive, or deeply serious spiritual health results.

Emotional Wellness

This is the "feeling" dimension of our well-being, and often, one of the dimensions most in need of development and balancing for many people. When we have this dimension in balance, we are able to honestly self-describe ourselves as stable or mature.

Take a moment in self-assessment. *Can you call your actions mature when you are hurt, embarrassed or feeling down?* Do you have the tools to improve your mood when you feel down, and do it in a healthy way?

Can you manage your emotions, or do you become confused, frightened or scared by what seems to be their power over you?

Are you fully present in your awareness of your state of mind… whether happy, sad, depressed or disengaged? *Are you emotionally stable?*

What supports that stability? *Does it come from the inside-out, or the outside-in…* where you depend on alcohol, pharmaceuticals, or illicit drugs to help you feel normal? Do you engage in high-risk behaviors?

Do you typically feel connected, or alienated from, the world around you? Do you feel at peace, or do you struggle with uncontrollable stress, which colors your interactions with yourself, and with others?

Environmental Wellness

This dimension encompasses your awareness of toxic substances, your *carbon footprint*, and your willingness to recognize the importance of, and care for the natural world around you. *Do you recycle, reuse and renew items you use on a regular basis?*

We are, all of us, stewards for this homeland.

Physical Wellness

Naturally this dimension includes your exercise and nutritional behaviors, sleep behaviors, and stress management skills.

In this dimension we typically consider our fitness level and willingness to commit to improving it if it has not been taken seriously in our lives, including: general nutritional status, eating habits, tobacco use, moderation in drinking, and abstinence from the use of illicit and misuse or abuse of over-the-counter drugs or pharmaceuticals.

Other aspects of self-care resident in this dimension include: adequate sleep, safe sexual behaviors, and regular physical, dental, and eye exams.

Occupational Wellness

This dimension of health is concerned with a number of factors that, as with any of the others, can enhance or hurt our well-being… for instance: does your job give you a sense of meaningful personal and financial *fulfillment*?

Is there healthy communication between you and management? Is there room for growth or promotion for you? Does the job offer opportunities to further your education? Do you feel that your work is valuable?

Social Wellness

Interestingly, many people rate themselves high on this dimension, because they don't fully understand it. **You are socially healthy if you feel comfortable in new social environments.**

You are confident in yourself, and know you understand how to develop and nurture friendships and other kinds of relationships in your life. You are a wise communicator. You are adept at resolving conflicts that arise in your life. You enhance the experiences of others.

All these dimensions are woven together in the tapestry that is our life.

> *Author's Note:*
> "We have often, in the course of delivering these materials in class, gathered data from our students, in the interest of better understanding which of these dimensions present a challenge, and which don't.
>
> Perhaps not surprisingly, the easiest of these dimensions to bring into balance are the mental and the physical. The hardest, the emotional and social dimensions.
>
> *Why?* **Because with discipline, we can train into our mental and physical health.**
>
> On the other hand, our emotional and social health is often subject to ingrained behaviors. Patterns, habits that powerfully direct how we act and react. Sometimes in healthy, sometimes in unhealthy ways… but often triggered in an almost autonomous way.
>
> *The suggestion here, consistently, is that the difficult is difficult because of our relative inability to communicate… with others, but more importantly, with ourselves.*
>
> Changing this, bringing this into balance through mindful awareness, is a perfect example of what fully integrating all of these dimensions is all about."
>
> *–JW*

It all begins with us, this balancing act... this inside job. This life's journey that, as we learn from 6th century philosopher Lao Tzu in his Tao Te Ching (*The Book of the Way*):

> *"The journey of a thousand miles begins with a single step."*

CHAPTER 3
The Spiritual Lens of Perception

SPIRITUAL AWAKENING
The mindful path of non-duality.

Without our ever noticing, the concept of **duality** not only lives among us, but often highly colors our correctness of our decisions, and the authenticity of our world view. **Good and bad, right and wrong**, for instance, *are really basic, integral concepts in our daily lives.*

This boxes us into an either/or, monochromatic world. *But if we listen to both, we begin to grow into a much different and **non-dualistic** understanding...* one which allows us to better recognize how we communicate with ourselves, and others.

Take a quick self-assessment moment here. When you hear others' opinions in casual conversation, what is typical to your responses? *Think about it for a moment.* Are you defensive and argumentative because you don't share their viewpoint, or are you open-minded and open-hearted?

The importance of recognizing how we relate to the world... dualistically or non-dualistically... *is an important step in birthing your conscious spiritual development.* If we skip this step, chances are we're missing out on a bigger picture.

Opinion, preference, and judgment aside, non-duality embraces the fundamental oneness of humanity. If you want to confirm that, observe any infant as it relates to the world in a completely non-differentiated way. Anger, intolerance, hatred *are all learned modalities, completely apart and distinct from the separation of duality.*

On its face, these two concepts live and breathe within theological practice and discussion. In the Christian tradition, for example, God is good. Satan is evil. Duality personified.

But in examining Scripture, it is relatively easy to discern that the duality here is misconstrued because it tells us several things in no uncertain terms:

God created him (Satan). Scripture proclaims all things were created by God and for God.
(ref. Rom 11:36; 1 Cor. 8:6; Col. 1:16–17)

God created him good. God only creates what's consistent with his/her nature—things that are themselves good. And in the beginning, whether in Heaven or here on Earth … everything was "very good."

(ref. 1 Tim. 4:4; 1 John 1:5; James 1:13)

In other words, it's all good, so no duality exists.

Non-duality then, *sees and experiences this world from a perspective of unitive consciousness, and all of the world's great wisdom teachers* spoke and lived in that consciousness: Lao Tzu, Buddha, Jesus, Gandhi, and many others. That this is possible is only underlined by this having been achieved all over the world, and across so many wisdom paths.

Of course, our choosing to grow spiritually is, in fact, *a choice,* but without this perception of oneness or unitive consciousness, we typically remain forever at odds with the world around us.

The dual-mind can also be recognized as the ego-mind. One that will continue to see the world as either black or white, good or evil and at the mercy of its own judgments and opinions. We really encourage you to investigate how this wants to play out in your life, and that an open-hearted curiosity will prevail.

RELIGION AND SPIRITUALITY
Differences and Similarities.

Let's preface and frame this dialogue with a few working definitions:

Religion is a commitment or devotion to a personalized, or institutionalized system of religious attitudes, beliefs and practices, which are used to worship a god or a group of gods.

Spirituality is a commitment to connecting with something bigger than ourselves, of which we are an inextricable, eternal part. It is a universal human experience that promotes an awareness of the complete inter-connectedness of life.

It is helpful when approaching this topic to look at historically accepted differences in these two modes of being in the world. It is also worth looking at their commonalities… areas where there is crossover between the two. The fact that there *is* crossover makes this a more challenging exercise but knowing that can serve to deepen our understanding.

Differences

Let's take a look at some of the ways in which the two have commonly been parsed out:

Religion	Spirituality
Divides/Separates	Unifies
Dogmatic	Ineffable
Exclusive	Inclusive
Exterior Work	Interior Work
Exteriorized Values	Internalized Values
Limiting	Expansive
Text-Centered	Heart-Centered

The first three characteristics listed here are somewhat inextricable… each plays with the others as an interdependent partner.

*Because religion is largely **dogmatic**,* i.e., inclined to lay down its beliefs, principles and practices as incontrovertibly true and invariably right, *it can be **exclusive*** in its lack of acceptance of the beliefs and principles of other religions. *Because religion can be **exclusive**, it runs the risk of being **divisive**,* acting to separate other religions from legitimacy because their "operating system" is, in its details, not the same as theirs.

Spirituality, on the other hand, *celebrates the **unity** in all of life*. Because of this open and expansive world-view, *it is **inclusive** of all sentient beings,* celebrating similarities rather than rejecting differences. *Because it is **inclusive**,* the spiritual world view focuses on the indescribable (**ineffable**) wonder of life rather than the rigidity of religious dogma.

The next several distinctions, **exterior vs. interior work**, and **exterior vs. interior values** are also inter-connected, and the latter is conditional on the former.

Exterior work is largely directed by introduction to **dogma** *and developing a relationship with it* where the work often rests with familiarizing and beginning to resonate with the concepts, tenets and practices of a religious world view. That world view may or may not have evolved over millenia. If not, it can run the risk of adherence to values, which may have significantly less meaning in contemporary society as they did in both the times and the culture in which they first came into practice.

Spirituality asks us to look inside, to do the **interior work** we need to do ourselves in order to better understand what our personal motivations are. *If we are all connected, how do we want to be present to that?*

This work, *interior and exterior*, **defines what our values are,** *and the way in which they are defined.* **One approach often defines our values for us, the other, through personal reflection and discernment.**

Because of these differences, **religion can often impose a limiting outlook on life,** by virtue of its adherence to its own dogma. **Spirituality, on the other hand, is expansive in its outlook,** as its affinity for self-examination leaves one increasingly more mindful over time of the unity of life, and of our inter-connectedness with each other, our planet, and our known universe.

The last of our initial distinctions here, **text-centered** vs. **heart-centered** asserts that, while **religion** is capable of evolving within a contemporary culture, it **remains largely dependent in its outlook on historical, and in many case, anecdotal writings**.

Spirituality is heart-centered in that its core demand is that we engage in personal exploration in the now. In looking at the light and the shadow within us, how that colors how we look at the world, and how to develop a mindful balance between the two, so that we are open to communicate, seeking common ground and learning to discuss areas of differing ideology. There is a potential for both individual expression, and an intellectual/emotional freedom with a heart-centered perspective.

Similarities and Points of Overlap

Increasingly, several models continue to evolve and emerge on the issue of religion and spirituality.

Some continue to see the two as dualistic and distinct, without any personally meaningful overlap. This is a place where communication is difficult, if not often impossible, because it suggests that religion and spirituality are each vying for audience attention, and that proselytizing is the only real goal of each. This is unfortunately first-order thinking, suggesting that there is a "right" and a "wrong" and that a choice must be made. Communication within this paradigm is extremely difficult. How many misunderstandings, how many arguments have you started in your life by adopting that approach? How many wars?

Others see religion and spirituality as two dimensions of one continuum, one reality, where each is with open heart searching for greater meaning in life. These two constructs can then co-exist, because it can accept that there are similarities and conceptual overlaps which invite, rather than dissuade communication.

So, what are some of the elements within this religious/spiritual continuum that begin to invite open-hearted communication?

One is **belief.** The belief in something greater. This "greater thing" takes many shapes and many names but is universally acknowledged as something in which we want, often need, to believe. Religion may more often see this source as something which is **external** to us. Spirituality more often sees it as **in** us. The important point of coherence is that there is a belief that there is something greater than us, which represents that there is reason for all that is, and by extension, purpose for and sanctity in all that lives.

Another is our **desire for connection**. Many of us seek relationship in our lives, as they are often, when well-nourished, of great comfort, and incubators for personal and emotional growth. We are no different in this desire for connection with something greater. Religion over centuries may have suggested that this connection is "the right thing to do," and that not having it may bring dire consequences. Spirituality asks us first to connect with, and love ourselves, and then to foster that self-love among others.

there
can peace
be
no — without
understanding.

- Senegalese proverb

A third is a healthy sense of **awe and respect for the ineffable**. The more that science advances, the more likely it has become that reality is an "inside job," one that we each have an ability to construct, but that is at best an approximation of what is really there... the true reality that is truly beyond our ability to sense, or even reason.

Another is our basic need **to develop deeper, richer meaning in life**. The ways, the means, the practices and rituals that we use as we strive for this may differ significantly. Some may be rigid, others less so. Some may take form in prayer to a greater source that is seen as external to us. Others may strive to bring increased focus and presence to the source, the light within us. Regardless, the desire is there.

Lastly, we have the need to know, if this is our only life, or if there are in fact many more to follow... **what is right living?** Both religion and spirituality seek this answer. They both seek to know what the path is to personal meaning, to a true connection with a greater source, to happiness.

At the end of the day, it seems right that we **do** look at religion and spirituality, and how they both exist in some sort of mystical, intertwined partnership, as beautiful expressions of our need for connectedness with the One... that source which is uniquely expressed in each of us.

How we validate that for ourselves is our choice. Through the inner search of spirituality, or through the dualistic teachings of the world's great wisdom paths. The two are not mutually exclusive, and both are there for us in this present moment—that one moment which matters most.

WHAT IS THE SOUL?
The uniquely expressed breath of life.

The Soul, and what it is, has been a topic of discussion for centuries.

The word itself has a long heritage on its way to our modern English... a translation of the Greek word "psyche" into the German word "sela," and to the old English word "sawol" on its way to our present day spelling.

Meanings of the word are many, but there is a general consensus that it is meant to refer to the uniquely expressed qualities of our inner life... *who we are at our core.*

Here's a few thoughts from those who have given it more than a little consideration as a part of their life's work:

Gary Zukav

The soul is that part of you that existed before you were born and that will exist after you die. It's the highest, most noble part of yourself that you can reach for.

Iyanla Vanzant

The soul, I believe, is the fingerprint of God that becomes a physical body. I believe that. It's the fingerprint... it's unique to everybody.

Deepak Chopra

The soul is the core of your being. It is eternal. It doesn't exist in space/time. It's a field of infinite possibilities, infinite creativity. It's your internal reference point with which you should always be in touch.

DeVon Franklin

The soul is the spirit. It is the connecting line to God. I believe the soul is where the Holy Spirit resides. I believe that it is literally, you know, when you pick up the phone and then you have your 4G network? The soul is the 4G network right to Heaven to me.

Daniel Pink

The soul is, I think, our capacity to see that our lives are about something more than simply the day to day, and that we're here for a purpose. It could be connected to religion or not, but that there is a purpose of your being here.

Debbie Ford

To me, the soul is a part of us that never dies. It's who we are at our core. And it carries all the messages and the lessons that we've learned in the past, and will carry all the lessons and the messages that we will carry into the future.

Eckhart Tolle

The soul is your innermost being. The presence that you are which is beyond form. The consciousness that you are beyond form, that is the soul. That is who you are in essence.

Michael Singer

The indwelling consciousness that watches the mind come and go. That watches the heart come and go, the emotions of the heart. And watches the world pass before you. You, the conscious, the consciousness, the center of being, is soul.

Wayne Dyer

The soul is the birthless, deathless, changeless part of us. The part of us that looks out from behind our eyes and has no form. The soul is infinite so there is no in or out of it. It is everywhere. There's no place that it is not.

Marianne Williamson

For me, it's the truth of who we are. The light, the love which is within us goes by different names, but the truth of us. Michelangelo said when he got a statue that he would go to the quarry and get a big piece of marble and the way he imagined it, God had already created the statue, and his job was just to get rid of the excess marble.

So that's what we're like. Inside is the being that God has already created. Some call it the Christ, the Buddha mind, the Shekinah, the light, the soul. And our job is to get rid of this excess—useless fear, thought forms of the world—that actually hide the light of the soul.

Llewellyn Vaughan-Lee

The soul is a Divine part of our self. It is our Divine nature. It is a part of us that is one with God. Everybody has a soul. It is the immortal internal part of ourselves. It never dies. It's immortal. It belongs to God.

Jean Houston

I believe that the soul is the essence of who and what we are. I personally believe that it transcends our leaving this mortal coil. And I think it comes with codes, and possibilities, and the next layers of who and what we may yet be. It is often a pain in the neck because it says: 'Wake up. It's time to wake up. Don't go to sleep.' I think it is also the lure of our becoming. That's what I think the soul is.

Is Spirit A Different Thing?

Much of its contemporary meaning has been colored by religious dogma, to the point where its usage in conversation today has decreased significantly and prompting a new acronym for the times, where young adults increasingly identify themselves as "spiritual, but not religious," or "SBNR," because conversations about the spirit are often no longer comfortable for many. ***But spirituality is on the rise.***

If we can for the moment accept these several definitions of what spirituality is:

- a deep sense of peace and well-being based on our interconnectedness
- a deep sense of wonder about the Universe

…then we can see in recent studies from the Pew Research Center that spirituality **is** on the rise, and it is on the rise particularly in GenXers and Millenials, and that these are their most commonly referred to definitions.

What then is Spirit? The root word in Latin is inspiritus, or, to be inspired.

Some would suggest that Spirit is the life force within us that expresses itself as our soul in its own unique way. Something that uniquely *feeds* the soul. Michael Meade has suggested, based on the teachings of the Vedas, ancient Hindu scriptures *that say it is our Soul that makes us each uniquely separate and distinct from the next.*

Are Soul and Spirit the same, then?

There is some consensus in the Abrahamic religions (Judaism, Christianity, and Islam) that Spirit is "the breath of God." To those who categorize themselves more as SBNRs, Spirit is more likely defined as the Universe expressed in each of us. The unique expression of that Spirit, that which defines us for ourselves and to others, may be more likely defined as our Soul, which may live on beyond this life as both Spirit (energy) and Soul (consciousness).

Religion has served to validate this outcome for us as a rite of passage.

However, we live in the passageway. And it is in the passage that so many have felt increasing comfort in our spiritual connectedness. And so, with increasing tension in our world, there is a tendency for us to gravitate towards one path or another, religious, or spiritual. *They are not mutually exclusive.* One path focuses on outcomes that are based on right living. The other, on the present, and our community with all living things, knowing that energy flows between it all, and perhaps that it somehow expresses a unified consciousness.

JOURNALING ASSIGNMENT 3.1

Take as much time as you need now to reflect on what soul means to you. *See if you can boil it down to a brief definition, such as the ones we've referenced above.*

_____

_____

_____

_____

_____

_____

It's likely that one of the definitions we've offered above resonated with you more than the others. *Which one was it, and why?*

_____

_____

_____

_____

_____

_____

IMPERMANENCE
Some spiritual food for thought.

> *"It is not impermanence that makes us suffer.*
> *What makes us suffer is wanting things*
> *to be permanent when they are not."*
>
> -Thich Nhat Hahn

> *"If we can see the miracle of one small flower, clearly*
> *our entire life would change in that instant."*
>
> -Constance McClain

Here's a question for you. The answer may seem simple enough, but it is a question that is a vital inquiry in opening up your spiritual path:

What can you think of that has permanence in life?

Your initial reaction was probably: **nothing**. If so, take a few moments to validate this a little bit further. As is always a good idea, start with yourself, and expand out from there:

Will I die?
Are my clothes going to last forever?
Will my pets, family members, friends always be in my life?
Is my home always going to be there?
Is my earth, this natural world, permanent?

Your answer is most likely still "no."

This notion of impermanence is a concept that is central to much of Eastern wisdom teachings, most notably Buddhism. *That life is finite.* It suggests that, once we let go of the human illusion of 'forever,' we are much better equipped to deal with reality. And the reality is that *life is lived, and life unfolds in the present moment,* so it's best to be present to each and every moment for which we are awake. In Buddhism, this concept is called 'anicca' *and asserts that all of existence, without exception, is transient,* and that accepting this allows us to begin to see things as they really are.

Here's a few other questions to consider along these same lines:
How many moments of my lifetime have I missed so far?
How many memories did I once have that have already disappeared?

These questions are rich grist for the mill... food for thought... and a powerful validation that the Eastern concept of mindfulness is a practice which can deeply enrich our lives in the moment. After all, that's all we really have.

When we fully realize the impermanence of life on Earth, we see and accept that everything, including ourselves and all that we love, will one day pass away from this life. *The beauty in this realization of impermanence opens up for us the miracle of compassion.* When we fearlessly take impermanence to heart we are gifted with a profound lesson that will inspire and guide us.

Recognizing the impermanence of life narrows the separation between others and ourselves. Once we recognize that everyone and everything is affected in the same matter, we cannot help but respond with a deep caring. With the recognition of the impermanent world comes great compassion, genuine care. Our minds open their potential fullness to love and appreciation.

As our compassion expands, it jogs our minds to recognize the grand nature of life. We glimpse the true nature of this world that lies beyond all our concepts of it. Suffering and pain become catalysts for a deeply felt sense of loving care in an unbiased way.

Our last comment on this topic is prompted by the writings of the highly revered spiritual teacher Ram Dass, who offers us some additional food for thought.

And that is simply this: if anything at all is in fact permanent, *it is our inner world of spirit...* that moves us away from our individual, compartmentalized bodies and thoughts... and towards a place where we can all become one with all that is, ever was or ever will be. *A place he calls home.*

And it is that road we choose to walk, towards our engagement with the infinite, which has inspired one of his most beloved quotes:

"We're all just walking each other home."

-Ram Dass

OUR INTERNAL COMPASS
Honoring our inner voice.

"Your vision will become clear only when you can look into your own heart.
Who looks outside, dreams. Who looks inside, awakes."

-Carl Jung

It is **genius** that, as human beings, we have been gifted with the ability to *feel into our experience...* that ping of like or dislike upon meeting someone or something new.

And it again was Swiss psychiatrist Carl Jung who gave us this profound insight that puts that ability, particularly with regard to new people in our lives, into its likely most proper perspective:

"Everything that irritates us about others can lead us
to an understanding of ourselves."

We can take this as axiomatic, *and it shows us our internal compass at work.* The task at hand then, is to raise our awareness to honor that inner voice... that compass which guides us so reliably in the unknown waters of new experiences in our life.

If we choose to more closely align with our spiritual selves, and trust that our compass always points true north, then our willingness to first thoroughly self-assess, *without ego attachments, or judgments borne of habit,* is critical.

How do we begin? Journaling is often a handy tool for this process. Write down those things, perhaps as a result of a peer review (a mindful conversation) with someone you trust, which are perceived by others as judgmental, prejudicial or biased. These are the things which you may or may not genuinely own, but regardless, they can often remain hidden from our awareness by the protective shield of our ego.

It's important in this process that we steer clear of guilt and self-loathing. The purpose of this is not to lay blame on ourselves, or anyone else. This purpose is to take an inventory, mindfully and with the greatest of self-care, so that we can take a step back from our baggage, and see ourselves with a sacred grace, and a clear vision for a better self.

the mind
is everything. what you
think, you become.

- Buddha

Listening to who we really are is a study in courage. It asks that we take a serious look at several aspects of our humanity that many would choose to ignore: *the degree of our narcissistic ego involvement, and the degree of our self-confidence, as expressed in the way we live our world.*

These are really two sides of the same coin.

Our ego involvement can easily cloud our vision to the world, and all of our relationships with it. In the extreme, *an ego inflated to the degree of narcissism* can almost completely mask our ability to see, or genuinely feel into everything with which we interact.

On the other side of this coin we find the portrait of our insecurity. Insecurities run rampant in our lives, and those who would suggest that they have none, well, they're just not being honest with themselves.

These are our initial challenges in honoring our true inner voice.

Reflect on it. Meditate on it. Watch carefully for what arises, without bringing emotion into the internal conversation.

Journal about it. Write down any and all the insecurities you've felt throughout your life. Begin at the beginning, with your earliest childhood memories. The insights you will gain will be amazing. Accept them with a generous, forgiving heart.

As you continue to travel down the path towards your highest self, you will continue to understand, and appreciate from your own unique perspective, that your spiritual development is best nurtured by your own sense of Divine honesty with, and sacred trust in… yourself.

To become spiritually alive is to genuinely surrender ourselves to a something greater than ourselves. Something we may never see. Except perhaps, if we choose to look in the mirror, and see how our light shines from within us, and out into the world.

YOUR SPIRITUAL AUTOBIOGRAPHY
Some thoughts on getting started.

For everything, there is a first time. And so, we'll begin at the beginning. Writing your spiritual autobiography may sound like an overwhelming task on first consideration. Many of us have never given it much, if any thought.

So, first things first. Exactly what is a spiritual autobiography?

Among other things, we believe that you'll find it to be a powerful tool in support of more mindfully, and more consistently bringing spirituality into your life. And so, it's not exactly your garden-variety autobiography, but one which will probably turn out to be something much, much more… both liberating and exciting for you in terms of making a heartfelt connection to your own life experience.

Life happens so quickly, and it keeps on coming, sometimes at breakneck speed, so it can often be easy to overlook those poignant, mystical moments we've already experienced, that can become important reference points for you as you continue on your journey.

We highly recommend going into this process in seclusion from what may be your everyday life: the distractions that so easily come from media and other minds. We respect the love you most probably have for music, TV, internet, friends, and family, but it's enormously helpful to walk away from them all, with gratitude that they are all a part of your life, for this exercise.

Begin to draw focus on how, if at all, something greater is, and has been at play in your life. You'll find that in this process of simply drawing attention to the inexplicable in your life those moments that have been formative and yet over which you have had no control will start to emerge for you.

The goal here is not to try to make this a comprehensive journal, but rather more of a selective reflection on those moments, events, periods of time, unexpected influences, provocative people, and unexplainable experiences about which you are led to write.

Be willing to be honest. This isn't about sharing the experience with anyone else. It's about sharing it with yourself, and then taking the time to first reflect upon what you've written, and then it all into a deeper discernment in search of honest, detached meaning.

This may not be a fairy tale experience. We are all beings of light, but the truth is, light casts shadows. So be prepared to see and experience both. They are both a part of you, and they can be brought into mindful, constructive balance.

Here's a few suggestions on ways that you can organize your approach to this.

A Thematic Approach

Here's some examples of a thematic approach to this process. Use any of these questions that are of interest to you, and if none of them particularly resonate with you, perhaps they will help you arrive at a personalized set that is both more comfortable and meaningful for you.

If you follow, or have followed a religious tradition:

- How has that shaped your life?
- Your perspectives on yourself, friends, family?
- The way you experience your inner and outer worlds?
- What has been good and bad about it?
- Have you adopted this tradition to the exclusion of accepting others?

Have you had an encounter, or encounters with something inexplicable? Call it Spirit, Source, God, but an experience for which you have no explanation?

- Was it a positive, or a negative one?
- If negative, do you believe the experience can change for the better?
- If so, how?
- How do you feel about making a commitment to that change?

Write about what you believe have been the most defining moments in your life so far. Moments that have shaped you, and that may have shaped the way in which you consider the importance of spirituality in your life.

Write about the people who have changed your life.

- Why were they influential?
- In what way were they influential?
- Did each change your life in a positive way?
- How? If not, how?
- Why is their influence so strong that it has shaped who you are today?

Devotion is also something to consider in your spiritual autobiography. Devotion often implies a commitment to a spiritual or religious icon. *But be careful here.* You may at first blush think that you've never been a devotional sort of person. If that is the case, consider some of these non-religious, non-spiritual objects of devotion:

- Your bicycle
- Your car
- Your pet
- Your friend
- Your favorite song

And so, in consideration those examples, have you had a devotional life?

- Who or what has shaped it?
- Is it important and integral to your daily life today?
- How does that take shape in your day?
- What impact has it had on you?

Is a mindful relationship with life trending for you right now?

- To what degree, and in what direction does it seem to be trending?
- Are you asking questions and pursuing answers to difficult questions?
- What are some of them?
- If so, does it represent growth and transformation in your life?

A Historical Approach

Here we can look at periods of time in your life. How you organize them is up to you. The closer we are to our early youth, the more conscious memory those periods can often carry. So, one way to approach this historically is to look at chunks of time... ten years each, for example... going back as far as you are able to remember.

Another approach would be to look at those moments in time where some significant shift occurred. Marriage, significant others, births, deaths, jobs... times of greatest joy or greatest sorrow.

Once you've identified those, think about what wrapped those events, before and after, and how the time surrounding each shaped you.

Journaling Assignment 3.2

Begin Writing

You now have some tools with which to begin chronicling your journey. Your spiritual journey. The ways in which all of these life-changing events have changed the way in which you perceive yourself, and the world around you.

Once you've finished, consider adding a few last words about where you think this is all leading for you, and how you want your life to grow with the seeds you plant today. What needs to happen in order for that vision of the future to become manifest?

Most importantly, consider this your first full-blown exercise in journaling. One which will provide you with a lasting reference point for many years to come. Read through it periodically, and notice how reading it makes you feel, and if it continues to give you insights into who you are in the moment you've chosen to re-visit it.

Thanks for making this investment in yourself, and never forget... we are, all of us... works in progress!

CULTIVATING THE HEART
Our Primary Organ of Perception.

Tucked in behind the sturdy armor of our rib cage. Protected from ancient weapons. But not protected from the often life-shattering emotional experiences that life may deal us.

Our heart serves us in a number of mysterious ways, and two of the most miraculous are that it nourishes us continuously, as it efficiently pumps oxygen-rich, life-giving blood through our bodies, while acting as a tender, but powerful 'holding space' for the wide range of emotions that can affect us at our very core, impacting our sense of well-being in both positive and negative ways.

The heart, and the efficiency with which it pumps blood, is regulated by our autonomic nervous system, so literally, that's a no-brainer.

But the ways in, and the efficiency with which it also acts as a processing center for our emotional and spiritual health is quite a different story.

In matters of emotion, which can so dramatically affect our spiritual health, the relationship between the heart and the brain is not so simple. Every event for which we have an emotional response, and for which our heart holds emotional space, requires processing not only the event, but all of the feelings associated with them, moment by moment, step by step.

This excerpt from a 1997 HeartMath Institute study (Science of the Heart: Exploring the Role of the Heart in Human Performance) offers a great description of this highly involved, highly evolved heart/mind communication:

"The study of communication pathways between the head and heart has been approached from a rather one-sided perspective, with scientists focusing primarily on the heart's responses to the brain's commands. We have learned, however, that communication between the heart and brain actually is a dynamic, ongoing, two-way dialogue, with each organ continuously influencing the other's function.

Research has shown that the heart communicates to the brain in four major ways: **neurologically** *(through the transmission of nerve impulses),* **biochemically** *(via hormones and neurotransmitters),* **biophysically** *(through pressure waves) and* **energetically** *(through electromagnetic field interactions).*

when a thing disturbs the peace of your heart, GIVE IT UP.

- Muhammed

Communication along all these conduits significantly affects the brain's activity. Moreover, our research shows that messages the heart sends to the brain also can affect performance."

From this, it's worth considering that how well the heart deals with its emotional challenges is at least, if not more important than how it deals with its physical ones, dealing moment by moment, in real time, with any of all of these powerful emotions: fear, anger, sadness, joy, disgust, trust, anticipation, surprise, and most importantly, love. A daunting, and sometimes overwhelming task.

Our heart feels. And good or bad, it can influence the entire state of our being, and the decisions we make based upon those states.

On a consistent, or even chronic basis, these powerful emotional stressors can exceed our ability to endure them, and the effectiveness of our communication with ourselves and with others changes, often to the point of our becoming emotionally as well as physically ill, as this powerful heart-centered communication system of ours begins to break down.

When that happens, we can find ourselves capable of what we might previously thought of as the unthinkable. A dark side emerges. If we have been hurt, we now lash out against those who have hurt us. If we mourn, we find ourselves in the dark, hopeless depths of despair, as we grieve for a lost beloved that once filled our life with joy.

We need only look so far as our own heart to notice how these emotions have been fully present. Our hearts are incredibly sensitive organs of perception, as well as powerful communication centers throughout our physiology. The good news is that we can learn, through our consistent practice, the power of our emotions on our physical health.

Try this experiment out for yourself to recognize this in your own body.

Cultivating Body/Heart Peace – a brief (20 minute) exercise

Here's a very short, simple exercise for you to try if you find that your heart is working too hard in the moment in supporting your needs for emotional balance and care.

Sit in a quiet space, one likely to remain free of interruptions, for about 20 minutes.

Draw your full awareness on the center of your chest, sitting tall, taking full, easeful breaths, breath by breath by breath.

Feel the calm flow of the air upon your skin, as it circulates all over your body, soothing you.

Now, in this more relaxed state, bring to mind something which brings you the emotion of sadness.

As you bring that thought or image into consciousness, pay attention to the signals your body is receiving. *Are you feeling any dis-ease in your body or mind? Make a mental note, if so.*

Now, return to your breathing as before. Let the thought or image go and return your awareness and focus to only your breathing. Sitting tall, taking full, easeful breaths.

Notice your heart-center. *How are you feeling now? Take a few moments to write about this experience. If you felt discomfort, or dis-ease with the image or thought, where did you feel it? Try to describe it. Once you were able to release that thought or image, did the discomfort go away?*

JOURNALING ASSIGNMENT 3.3

What are your thoughts on this heart/mind connection? Could this take its toll on your emotional, spiritual and physical health over time?

_____

_____

_____

_____

_____

_____

_____

_____

_____

_____

_____

_____

_____

_____

_____

_____

_____

_____

_____

_____

_____

_____

_____

_____

_____

_____

_____

_____

_____

AN EXAMINATION OF HEART CONSCIOUSNESS
Beginning to look back mindfully on our day.

We have opportunities every day to not only be aware of our heart, and our spiritual health, but to participate in spiritually heart-healthy activities. These may involve others, of course, but it's also important to remember that spiritual health "begins at home."

As the day winds down today, take a walk through this list, and make a few notes below, summarizing your spiritual health exercises for the day and how you feel after doing them.

JOURNALING ASSIGNMENT 3.4

Inspired by our colleague Jan Phillips and adapted with permission.

Did I say only kind words today?

Did I remember that my thoughts become my life?

Did I choose good thoughts?

Did I love my body?

Did I feel content?

Did I offer acceptance? Forgiveness?

Did I smile and laugh?

Did I reveal my light?

Did I notice the other's light?

Did I hug anyone?

Was I mindfully present in all my interactions and tasks?

Did I slow down enough to experience moments of bliss?

Did I look for Spirit? Divine Presence? God?

Am I thankful?

Did I express my appreciation?

Did I receive love? Did I give love?

Because I am love.

I am.

THOUGHTS ARE THINGS
The struggle to make them good ones.

One of the most powerful stressors on our spiritual health can be our own self-talk.

We have tremendous difficulty shutting down the incessant chatter in our minds, and the most impactful of these voices can be our negative thoughts and emotions. Even at moderate levels, it can be exhausting, draining our energy and challenging our self-confidence.

However, when they ramp up in frequency and intensity, the side-effects can be devastating. Negative thoughts and emotions can translate into a variety of emotions wanting to express, but for which there is no seeming outlet. The result is anxiety and can lead to depression, as well as self-destructive behavior, such as addiction. *And we begin to lose our way.*

We do have a choice. We can go down this road, or we can begin to be mindful that these thoughts and emotions exist and engage in a healthy dose of self-compassion. In doing so, we can redirect the negative chatter into positive. *It's still chatter, but it's a healthy start!*

There's an old legend, often attributed to the Cherokee, that illustrates this choice so beautifully. This choice between the good and bad inside us, that can either be expansive, or tragically self-limiting:

Two Wolves

An old Cherokee is teaching his grandson about life. "A fight is going on inside me," he said to the boy.

"It is a terrible fight and it is between two wolves. One is evil—he is anger, envy, sorrow, regret, greed, arrogance, self-pity, guilt, resentment, inferiority, lies, false pride, superiority, and ego."

He continued, "The other is good—he is joy, peace, love, hope, serenity, humility, kindness, benevolence, empathy, generosity, truth, compassion, and faith. The same fight is going on inside you—and inside every other person, too."
The grandson thought about it for a minute and then asked his grandfather, "Which wolf will win?"

The old Cherokee simply replied, "The one you feed."

Spend some time with the two wolves. *Which one are you feeding?* If you're feeding the evil one, ask yourself: *what good is this thought doing for me?*

Chances are the conclusion you'll come to is: not much, and that it's much more empowering to focus on the good, and on healthy outcomes for your life. We hope that you'll devote some time to this practice in pursuit of your spiritual consciousness and your heart/mind health.

Here's a few personal belief constructs that you might want to visit as you give this more thought:

Self-Limiting Beliefs	Life-Expanding Beliefs
Self-critic I am angry, negative, selfish, and self-centered.	**Self-Compassion** I affirm my value to myself and others, and I understand that everyone experiences similar changes.
Clinging I don't want to change how I live my life or engage in my relationships.	**Surrender** I surrender to changes that happen around me. I release my attachments.
Insecure stereotypes I look terrible. I have limited experience, extra weight, poor communication skills. I am undesirable, unattractive, and selfish. People must think poorly of me.	**Insecurity re-imagined** I let go of my attachment to negativity about myself and imagine my life unfolding in new ways that include wisdom, compassion, and peace.
Hopeless My life is useless. I have no purpose or value for my life.	**Meaningful** I continue to contribute value for myself and others. My life has meaning and purpose. I enrich the lives of others.

Fear of aging	Grace in aging
I don't like to be around someone who is sick or dying. I don't know what to say and I feel uncomfortable. It makes me depressed when someone I care about gets sick or dies.	I can be present with someone who is sick or dying. I do not have to fix or solve their problems. I can just be with them in all that arises, without fear. I can find the grace in every moment.
Holding grudges	**Forgiveness**
I have been wronged and disrespected. I can never forgive those that hurt or wronged me.	I am aware of the hold that cruel acts have had on me. I let go of this negativity so that I can move on in the beautiful flow of life.
Directionless	**Intentional**
I feel confused about life and aging. I don't know what I think about it.	My intention is to age well. I stand behind qualities and values that are important to me. I can and do make conscious choices about my aging.
Isolation	**Interconnection**
I am alone and separate from others. All my friends are gone. No one suffers from aging like I do. I am all alone now.	I am interconnected with the human family. I understand that my suffering reflects that of others as well, and that we all suffer. Being with others is important and nourishing to my life.

-modeled after IONS' Conscious Aging program

KNOWING THYSELF
Knowing what's true in your life.

"Rather than love, than money, than fame, give me truth."

-Henry David Thoreau

If you don't know what you're living for, you haven't lived yet.

- Rabbi Noah Weinberg

We are able, when we commit to being honest with ourselves, *to design an authentic life*. This process allows us to achieve clarity about what is important to us, about how we want to face out into the world. About what's true in our life, and about who we really are.

We begin designing ourselves by first identifying those most highly desirable attributes which either currently define us, or those which we want for us… the ones which we hold in the greatest possible esteem. **These values express themselves in a variety of ways,** as personality traits, by the lifestyles to which we aspire, and by the day-to-day choices we repeatedly make.

All of these combine at the highest level as **personality types,** which most personality tests serve to identify. *Let's examine these for a moment and determine with some confidence what our personality type is.*

Personality Types

The Meyers-Briggs Type Indicator is a personality screening tool in common use today. Its basic premise is that you are one of 16 possible personality types, based on the answers you provide to a battery of screening questions.

It is by no means the only test of this type that is currently out there and in use, and is only referenced here as an example of how personality types can be assessed.

We start with four questions, each one with two possible choices. Pick one choice for each question. Try not to spend too much time thinking about each one. Your most authentic choice comes from reading the descriptions, and easily self-identifying with the one which seems more natural to you.

Write your choices down, so that you remember them later:

Question 1: Are you outwardly or inwardly focused?
(which description describes you best?)

> Are you talkative and outgoing? Do you like to be in a fast-paced environment? Do you tend to work out ideas with others? Do you enjoy being the center of attention?

If so, then you prefer Extroversion. (E)

Are you reserved, or private? Do you prefer a slower pace? Do you tend to think things through to yourself? Would you rather observe than be the center of attention?

If so, then you prefer Introversion. (I)

Question 2: How do you prefer to absorb information?
(which description describes you best?)

By focusing on the reality of how things are? By paying attention to the facts and the details? Do you prefer ideas that have practical applications? Do you like to describe things in a literal way?

If so, then you prefer Sensing. (S)

Do you imagine the possibilities of things? Do you look at the big picture? Do you enjoy ideas and concepts for their own sake? Do you like to describe things in a poetic way?

If so, then you prefer Intuition. (I)

Question 3: How do you prefer to make decisions?
(which description describes you best?)

In an impersonal, logical way? Do you value justice and fairness? Do you enjoy finding the flaws in an argument? Are you often described as reasonable and level-headed?

If so, then you prefer Thinking. (T)

Do you base your decisions on personal values? Do you value harmony and forgiveness? Do you like to point out the best in others? Are you often described as warm or empathetic?

If so, then you prefer Feeling. (F)

Question 4: How do you prefer to live your outer life?
(which description describes you best?)

Do you prefer to have matters settled rather than up in the air? Do you think rules and deadlines should be respected? Do you prefer step-by-step instructions? When you make plans, do you want to know the details?

If so, then you prefer Judging. (J)

Do you prefer to leave your options open? Do you see rules and deadlines as flexible? Do you like to improvise and make things up as you go? Are you spontaneous, and do you enjoy surprises and new situations as they may arise in the moment?

If so, then you prefer Perceiving. (P)

Now, combine the four letters which represent the choices you've made, to see a more detailed description of yourself:

ISTJ Practical and fact-minded, extremely reliable.	**ISTP** Bold, yet practical experimenters, and masters with all kinds of equipment.
ISFJ Dedicated, warm protectors. Always ready to defend a loved one.	**ISFP** Flexible, charming artists. Always ready for something new.
INFJ Quiet, mystical. An inspiring and tireless idealist.	**INFP** Poetic, kind, and altruistic. Always ready to support a good cause.
INTJ An imaginative and strategic thinker, never without a plan.	**INTP** An innovator, with an unquenchable thirst for knowledge.
ESTP A sharp, energetic, and perceptive entrepreneur, who lives on the edge.	**ESTJ** An excellent administrator, unsurpassed at managing things and people.

ESFP	ESFJ
A spontaneous, energetic, and enthusiastic lover of life.	Extraordinarily caring, social, and popular.
ENFP	ENFJ
An enthusiastic, creative free spirit.	A charismatic and inspiring leader.
ENTP	ENTJ
A smart and curious thinker, always ready for an intellectual challenge.	A bold, imaginative, and strong-willed leader.

Interesting, yes? The Meyers-Briggs test is commonly used in corporations in the course of assessing new and prospective employees, because it can predictably profile an applicant's personality type and determine how well that matches with the position for which the applicant is applying.

Personality Traits

Within each of these **personality types**, by whatever means they are determined, any number of **personality traits** can exist in combination, some positive, some neutral and some negative.

The goal of our self-examination here is to do our best to honestly identify those traits which currently exist in us, those to which we aspire, and in doing so, improve our spiritual health.

Here are a few examples:

Positive
   Caring, Creative, Forgiving, Humorous, Insightful, Passionate, Reliable

Neutral
   Cerebral, Earthy, Intense, Mystical, Outspoken, Private

Negative
   Aggressive, Arrogant, Calculating, Dishonest, Fearful, Hateful, Narcissistic

Using these example personality traits, pick one from each group which best describes you. Then pick one from each group that best describes the traits to which you aspire.

Lifestyle Values

We can look at these as higher-level goals which we set for ourselves, which we adopt at a consistent, core level, and which serve to provide us focus through their inspirational and motivational power. Here are a few examples:

- Exercise as a way of life
- Eating healthy
- Adopting learning as a lifelong practice
- Developing your physical, emotional and spiritual health
- Valuing spiritually-aligned relationships
- Practicing open-hearted communication

Day-to-Day Choices

Our day-to-day lives give us a steady flow of opportunities for choice. Some are positive and support our physical, emotional, and spiritual health... others, less so. Here are a few examples of each:

Supportive

Being Present in the Moment, Dedicating Time to Meditation, Looking at Life as Opportunity, Seeking Friendships, Listening to Others, Sincerity in Relationships

Non-Supportive

Negativity with Others, Self-Sabotage, Inviting Stressful Situations, Substance Abuse, Making Self-Centered or Selfish Choices

JOURNALING ASSIGNMENT 3.5

Let's first take a look at what values are at your core… the ones that really drive you, and the ones you wish did. To help get you started, here's a list of values to look over. **Identify any and all with which you resonate** *(either the ones that you believe you currently embody, or those to which you aspire):*

Acceptance	Achievement	Adaptability	Ambition
Assertiveness	Attentiveness	Awareness	Balance
Bravery	Calm	Cleanliness	Clarity
Commitment	Communication	Compassion	Concentration
Confidence	Consistency	Control	Courage
Creativity	Curiosity	Dedication	Dependability
Devotion	Discipline	Drive	Empathy
Energy	Enthusiasm	Ethical	Expression
Family	Fame	Fearless	Fidelity
Focus	Freedom	Friendship	Giving
Grace	Gratitude	Happiness	Health
Honesty	Honor	Humility	Imagination
Independence	Individuality	Inspiring	Integrity
Intelligence	Intensity	Intuitive	Joy
Kindness	Leadership	Love	Loyalty
Motivation	Optimism	Originality	Passion
Patience	Peace	Power	Productivity
Prosperity	Purpose	Realistic	Reason
Respect	Responsibility	Reverence	Security
Self-reliance	Sensitivity	Serenity	Sincerity
Skill	Smart	Spirit	Spirituality
Spontaneous	Stability	Strength	Success
Support	Talent	Thankful	Thoughtful
Transparency	Understanding	Vision	Vitality
Wealth	Wisdom		

Next, create a list of your top ten values *(in no particular order of importance):*

Value 1 _____	Value 6 _____
Value 2 _____	Value 7 _____
Value 3 _____	Value 8 _____
Value 4 _____	Value 9 _____
Value 5 _____	Value 10 _____

Now that you have inventoried the values which you currently emulate, and perhaps some to which you aspire, *the next step in this exercise is to build upon that foundation, solidifying your values in your consciousness.*

Spend some time with each one. Be clear as to why each is important to you. *If any of them fail that test, re-assess.* Find another which better resonates for you.

Once you're satisfied with your list, write a brief, concise paragraph *describing* **why each individual value holds this deeply authentic importance for you.** *Why is this degree of clarity important?* Because these values, when authentically presented to the world, represent who you are, and what is important to you. *Values paint an unmistakable portrait of who we are.*

Once this first step is completed, take a few moments to prioritize your values. Rank them below in their personal importance to you, with 1 being most important, and 10 the least. **While doing this exercise, step outside of yourself and try to observe yourself looking at your thought process as you review each value.** *Why is this important?*

Because this is a self-evaluation, and when we undertake this for the first time, we are all capable of missing cues. Are these value choices really ours, or a simulation of someone else's? Do we hold them dear, or is it more important that others *believe* that they are to you?

As you re-assess and rank your values, do your best not to distort your perception of what you believe your truth to be. *The only real goal here is for you to become a more authentic individual, supported by personal values which hold real meaning for you:*

My Top 10 Values - Ranked *(1 = most important, 10 = least)*

#1 _____   #6 _____

#2 _____   #7 _____

#3 _____   #8 _____

#4 _____   #9 _____

#5 _____   #10 _____

REFLECTION AND DISCERNMENT
What differentiates the two practices of personal reflection and discernment?

While both of these practices bring dimension to our experiences, whether academic or experiential… *there are distinctions to be made between the two which are important*, so we'll take the opportunity now to define and differentiate the two.

Reflection

Reflection is a practice which helps us authentically form meaning from both our academic and experiential lives. We think, in retrospect, about what we've done, and what we've learned. It brings sunlight and clarity to our otherwise murky understandings. In this review we find deeper meaning, and we often discover if there are truths with which we resonate on a deeply personal level.

Reflection helps us realize more and more about ourselves, the current trajectory of our lives, and helps us frame them through a more spiritually alive lens. Without reflective inquiry, it can be relatively easily to forget lessons learned which might otherwise have significant meaning for our personal growth.

Discernment

When we take our reflections into *discernment,* we dig in deeper, to further uncover the spiritual treasure of our 'finds.' *Spiritual discernment then, means looking for something that is not easily seen… something beyond reflection.*

ANGER towards another steals our inner peace.

LETTING GO creates a bridge of reconciliation, peace and freedom.

- Constance McClain

Discernment allows us to know ourselves. It helps us complete the reflection process by better understanding who we are *before we assert that we know who others are*—before drawing conclusions and making judgments.

We take something into discernment, we take our reflections on our life experience, and determine if and how they resonate in the development of our personal values. As a practice, it means being honest and compassionate with ourselves, and setting our judgment of both ourselves and others aside.

YOUR WORLD VIEW
How it shapes your personal values.

When we begin to discuss how we perceive the world around us, and the worlds we carry around *within* us in our constantly chattering minds, we can begin to walk through the spiritual catacombs of our own design, along the way observing the intricate webs of opinions, prejudgments, and incorrect preconceptions which we have spun, all of which having colored our perception of our own value, and our ability to live in grace and in service to the *real* world.

Your Picture of the World.

When we begin unraveling this inner mindscape, this incredibly complex web which shapes our reality, we can see that, due to so many factors no two world views, and as such no two realities are exactly the same. From birth, we have internalized and synthesized an overwhelming amount of information, often without having the presence of mind to discern, or any reason to doubt.

Our earliest, most deeply ingrained influences on our world view most often rest with our families. The guidance, good or bad, of our parents. The infusion of moral, ethical and cultural values. The way we absorb the thoughts, beliefs, perceptions and opinions of siblings, relatives and friends. Our early academic education, so often represented as fact-based learning, but invariably colored by the world views of our teachers. All of this and more is internalized and re-cast as a world view that we want to believe is uniquely ours, but that is hardly the case.

SCIENCE is not only compatible with spirituality, it is a profound source of spirituality.

When we recognize our place in an immensity of light years and in the passage of ages, when we grasp the intricacy, beauty and subtlety of life, then that soaring feeling, that sense of elation and humility combined, is surely SPIRITUAL.

- Carl Sagan

In order for us to evolve into our own world view, it's important that we take the time to sit back and look into the mirror to begin to gain some clarity on what has shaped our lives, who has shaped our lives, and most importantly whether or not, on reflection, if we believe those influences are authentic, and spiritually healthy for us.

In this way, we can truly begin to lay a solid foundation for a life well-lived. A life whose trajectory, whose path going forward, is true to our uniquely personal vision. To begin means beginning to perceive the world through your most highly evolved organ of perception... your heart.

Whatever you find there which is not alive, erase. Give yourself the space for new experiences that can better, more authentically guide you down your own path. They are your best guides: they are yours, and yours alone.

And so, the Question is…

Where do I start? **With some reflective questions to jog the memory of your memory, of course!** When we're young, our developing brains are so pliable, so eager to **know**, that we bypass critical thinking in favor of absorbing information. So, in order to begin to construct our authentic world view, we need to return to our origins… that young age where our perceived beliefs reside.

*It will take some time and effort to first, remember what has shaped your existing world view, and second, to assess those beliefs to determine whether or not **you** actually hold them as true.* The benefit in the end is being able to look in the mirror, and see a spiritually free, authentic individual, free of preconception, and more highly focused on the present.

Your behavior may change in the process. Maybe slightly. Perhaps radically. Your spiritual authenticity will begin to manifest through your informed actions, the words with which you choose to communicate, and the activities you choose to spend your precious time in pursuing.

So, let's begin with a few questions. But before we do, try to dispel any discomfort that you might be feeling as you engage in this important reflection.

In your reflection, and more importantly, subsequent to it…it is important to steer away from blame, and to hold ourselves, as well as others who have contributed in some way to our development in highest respect for their traditions, teachings, and beliefs. They have wanted something for you, whether your realization of their dreams never fulfilled, or world views that have defined them: athletic or artistic pursuits, or their immersion in a sacred belief system.

You may come to find yourself at odds with others within the social circle of your development. That is a very normal outcome of this process, and it is important to remember that the world view which you have inherited comes honestly and has likely been based on the strongly-held beliefs of those who love you.

If you no longer share them, does that mean that you should no longer respect the source? *Hopefully, that is not the case.* They have, after all, gotten you this far in life.

Instead, why not place your new energetic focus on the blessings ahead of you? On the celebration of your authentic self, and the abundant, self-actualized[1] personal freedom you will begin to enjoy as a result of your hard work?

You are about to embark upon a truly personal journey. You may find that in the process, your spiritual development may come to differ from that of friends, family and loved ones, but in contrast, it can actually serve to deepen your appreciation in the diversity it now represents. It is not important to be right in your new world view. Only to know that it is authentic.

JOURNALING ASSIGNMENT 3.6

Do you believe in a higher power, God, Goddess, or a Source of all life?

If so, please write down as many reasons for your beliefs as possible. Was that belief given to you as a child? By whom, and in what ways? Did being in a religious sacred space... a church, synagogue, a mosque, or nature... and listening to what was being said piqued your curiosity on this issue?

_____

_____

_____

_____

Do you hold any prejudices, preconceptions or judgments?

If so, please write them down. How did you arrive at them? Who or what influenced these views or personal values?

_____

_____

_____

_____

_____

Do you feel a connection with other cultures and their traditions?

If so, please elaborate as to why you do. What world cultures and their traditions, or what sub-cultures of your own country resonate with you? Why? If you feel no connection, why? Are your feelings a result of meaningful history in your personal life, or are they a product of prevailing opinions?

_____

_____

_____

_____

_____

Do you feel a connection with other religions and their traditions which differ from your own?

If so, please journal why. To which of the world's great wisdom paths do you relate? Why? If you don't feel that you relate with any other than your own, why? Are those feelings genuinely yours, or do they reflect the opinions of others who may be, or who may have been influential in your life?

_____

_____

_____

_____

Do you feel the need to be right in communicating with others?

If so, please tell yourself why. Do you listen with the intent to respond, or with the intent to hear? Are the opinions, the world views of others, valid to you... or are they unimportant in relation to your own?

_____

_____

_____

_____

_____

These are the formative issues that have shaped your existing world view, and those which can re-shape it to your uniquely personal vision. You may have never previously had the opportunity to investigate why they are what they are. **If that's so**, please continue to bear in mind that there are no right or wrong answers, only authentic ones, and that the benefit that we gain from looking at our life with an open heart is one of the most impactful, far-reaching investigations that we can ever undertake in pursuit of our spiritual health.

CHAPTER 4
Deep Truths and Role Models

DIVINE PARADOXES
Seeming contradictions, deeper truths.

A paradox is a statement that combines several premises, each of which are true in and of themselves, which in their juxtaposition together lead to what seems at first an unacceptable conclusion, but which prove to be well-founded upon our deeper reflection.

One of the best examples of secular paradox has to be the entire opening paragraph of Charles Dickens' *A Tale of Two Cities*:

> *"It was the best of times, it was the worst of times,*
> *it was the age of wisdom, it was the age of foolishness,*
> *it was the epoch of belief, it was the epoch of incredulity,*
> *it was the season of light, it was the season of darkness,*
> *it was the spring of hope, it was the winter of despair."*

How can all of these things be true? Well, in this particular example, Dickens is describing life in two cities, London and Paris around the time of the French Revolution, and indeed, from different perspectives that could absolutely have been both a brilliant and accurate statement.

Divine paradoxes on the other hand, take us into a much deeper process of spiritual discernment, and ask us to examine their truth in our own lives.

Here is the Second Verse of the Tao Te Ching, an ancient, holy and paramount piece of writing attributed to Chinese philosopher Lao Tzu, a 6th century BC contemporary of Confucius:

Under heaven all can see beauty as beauty,
only because there is ugliness.
All can know good as good only because there is evil.
Being and non-being produce each other.
The difficult is born in the easy.
Long is defined by short, the high by the low.
Before and after go along with each other.
So the sage lives openly with apparent duality
and paradoxical unity.
The sage can act without effort
and teach without words.
Nurturing things without possessing them,
he works, but not for rewards;
he competes, but not for results.
When the work is done, it is forgotten.
That is why it lasts forever.

JOURNALING ASSIGNMENT 4.1

Choose one sentence from Lao Tzu's work above about which to briefly share your thoughts.
What is your interpretation of it, and what does it mean to you personally?

_____

_____

_____

_____

_____

_____

_____

_____

_____

WHO IS WISE?

one who learns from every man.

WHO IS STRONG?

ONE overpowers
WHO his inclinations.

WHO IS RICH?

One who satisfied with his lot.

WHO IS HONORABLE?

One who honors his fellows.

- Ben Zoma

EXEMPLARS
What are they, and why is it important for us to find them on our way to spiritual well-being?

Exemplars are our role models… **those who epitomize the** *spiritual characteristics* **we yearn to emulate in our own lives.**

It's not always easy to see, or even imagine our highest selves. Our world view reflects where we are now in the lifelong process of maturing, and we may for any number of reasons be blocked in the moment from evolving or even knowing that we need to continue. *Seeing our own potential, and our possibilities for becoming a more spiritually developed, evolved self, can be tricky.*

Unless we have an ideal example (an **exemplar**) with whom we choose to align, this dimension of ourselves, *perhaps the very best of us*, can often remain undeveloped. **We'd like to offer some examples from our own lives, to illustrate this for you.**

Your exemplars may be living or deceased. Famous, or not. Often, they are extraordinary, everyday people. The common thread is that they are either now, or at some time previously, powerful influencers.

Constance's Exemplar List

My list is so long that I will share only a partial list with you here, but please understand that, in taking the opportunity to look back over my life there have been many, many more.

I hold each of them in my heart as Divine Souls to whom I have gracefully been guided. I used to be an extremely willful young woman, but mercifully, through their guidance and leadership I have learned the importance and meaning of humility and service, and the possibilities in my life for right living.

Without my exemplars, all of them - I often pause to consider how my life would have easily dead-ended.

–CM

The Buddha

I became aware of the Buddha's teachings in my twenties. It was a time in my life when I read voraciously as many spiritually oriented books as I could find. *My pursuit of "Buddha Mind" continues to this day, forty years later!*

Thich Nhat Hahn

I was first introduced to this great teacher in 1985, when I was attracted to a book cover on a table in my best friend's house. It was Thich Nhat Hahn's *The Sun My Heart*. My generous friend and soulmate Matthew immediately said, "Take it, it's yours. I know you'll love it."

Love it I did, and I continue to learn from Thay (his nickname, pronounced 'tie'), to this day. This Vietnamese Zen Buddhist has offered me so many important life lessons that I have literally inhaled his writings ever since.

In 2006, I was fortunate to be in Thay's presence at his Deer Park monastery, just north of San Diego, California. Even before this exciting retreat with my beloved Buddhist master, I had come to feel his presence through his writings, and I wanted nothing more than to emulate his wisdom and teachings.

Jesus of Nazareth

I was introduced to God and Jesus by my non-religious mother when I was three. As with so many of us, I gained further knowledge about his life's journey through the Sunday school classes that I (sporadically) attended throughout my early grade school years.

By the ripe age of four or five, I began to pray to Him for the well-being of my family and friends, and for *"an important job"* to do in my life. I felt a great kinship with Jesus at this point in my life.

Mary Taylor

"Mare" was my mom's best friend, and the wife of my father's best friend… a public health nurse, and mother of five beautiful, talented children. Over time, Mary became, in her unique unobtrusive way, a second mother to me. My own mother was an alcoholic, and we never connected in the ways which were so deeply important to me.

Mary gave me that connection. I always felt her love for me, through her constant availability to me, both as a role model, and as a surrogate parent. That has become a deeply spiritual, supportive quality that I have chosen to emulate in my life ever since.

She and her husband Norm (cut of the same spiritual cloth) continued in this capacity throughout my life, after both my parents passed, until they did as well. To this day, I feel their unconditional love, wrapping me up in safety. I hope I also transmit this same energy to those of my students, clients, and friends who might need that same assurance.

Mary-Glenn Cromwell

Mary-Glenn, (otherwise known as "Hugs" to many) is a few years older than me, and one of those human beings who easily finds something to love in everyone she meets. Her ever-present grace has helped me envision that same possibility for my own life, and for that reason alone, she has had a huge impact on my spiritual evolution.

Saint Francis of Assisi

Saint Francis, was born in 1189 in Assisi, Italy, son of a wealthy merchant. As a young man he drank and partied a lot. After being jailed for a few years he emerged from that incarceration a changed man and began to preach in the Christian way. He was said to have heard God say to him: "rebuild the church." *Which he did.* Francis is the Patron Saint of animals, and of our ecology. *(Assisi is north of Rome, in the center of the very heart of Italy, and one of my favorite places on the planet).*

Mother Teresa

Mother Teresa of Calcutta was physically small in stature, but fiercely active in her missionary work with impoverished communities. In 1979 she won the Nobel Peace Prize for "for work undertaken in the struggle to overcome poverty and distress, which also constitutes a threat to peace."

Brother Wayne Teasdale

Brother Wayne was best known as an energetic proponent of mutual understanding between the world's religions, and for an interfaith dialogue, for which he coined the term *"interspirituality."* He was also an active campaigner on issues of social justice. Sadly, Brother Wayne passed away in 2004. He was 59 years old. His book ***The Mystic Heart*** is an important book for these uncertain times. *We highly recommend it.*

Father Thomas Keating

Father Thomas was a Trappist monk and priest, known as one of the architects of **centering prayer**, *a contemporary method of contemplative prayer*. We lost Father Thomas this year. He was 95 years young. He was a founder of the wonderful Colorado-based organization Contemplative Outreach Ltd, a spiritual network of individuals and small faith communities committed to living the contemplative dimension of the Gospel, and he has authored dozens of books on centering prayer and contemplative practices.

Brian Luke Seaward

Brian Luke Seaward first came to my attention when I was an instructor at the University of California, Santa Barbara. He had published some of his work of managing stress, which was of interest to me, but not centered on the topic of my primary interest, spiritual health.

Three years later, his book, *Spirituality and Health*, crossed my desk, and it felt like an act of Divine Intervention.

A year after that, I was asked to do a radio talk show in Santa Barbara. I knew I wanted a show on spirituality to help demystify the connections between spirituality and science, as it had become a new and exciting area of research. Brian Luke graciously agreed to be my first guest and the show was off to a wonderful start. His work has inspired me for twenty years since, and I am grateful for our chance meeting along the way.

Others you may wish to research include **Camille and Kabir Helminski** *(Sufi scholars of the Jalaledin Rumi lineage)*, **Jean Houston** *(an American writer whose writings are largely focused on human potential)*, **Cynthia Bourgeault** *(modern day mystic, Christian contemplative, and author of numerous books on contemplative practices and inter-spiritual dialogue)*, **Ed Bastian** *(founder of the Spiritual Paths Foundation, and co-author of the award-winning book 'Living Fully, Dying Well')* and **Joan Borysenko** *(a distinguished pioneer in integrative medicine, and a world-renowned expert in the mind/body connection)*.

Jim's Exemplar List

Upon taking my inventory, I found my list to be all over the place: from the highly spiritual, to those who would at first glance seem to be not so much. My wild guess is that I am by no means unique in that self-assessment.

The important thing is, not who is on the list, but more about what they have meant, or could mean to you.

Their being famous earns you no extra credit. Their being authentic in the life they have lived does.

That their work resonates with you, and that it spurs you on towards your best self does as well.

-JW

Bahá'u'lláh

As a young man growing up on the North Shore of Chicago, I discovered one weekend one of the most remarkable structures I have personally witnessed to this day... the Baha'i Temple in Wilmette, Illinois.

Members of the Baha'i faith believe that Bahá'u'lláh was the most recent of a series of Divine educators, including Abraham, Krishna, Zoroaster, Moses, Buddha, Jesus, and Muhammed, and that the religions of the world come from the same Source, and are in essence successive chapters of one religion from God.

Their vision is that the crucial need facing humanity is to find a unifying vision of the future of society and of the nature and purpose of life. As a young man, this was, and remains a concept around which I can wrap both my mind and heart.

Moses

For helping so many (and myself eventually) understand that the Sabbath is not only a great idea, but that it can be a life-changing spiritual practice. While in Judaism it is a practice to which an entire day a week is dedicated, I've found that from both a spiritual and a practical perspective… a "mini-Sabbath…" whether that may be ten minutes or several hours of dedicated rest (where we take what respite we can from our busy lives) has become a godsend. *Thank you, Moses.*

Mother Teresa

Once, Mother Teresa was asked how she could continue day after day after day, visiting the terminally ill: feeding them, wiping their brows, and giving them comfort as they lay dying… and she said: "It's not hard, because in each one, I see the face of Christ in one of His more distressing disguises." This is not an easy path, but it is one that opens one's heart in plain sight of our highest self, as we bear witness to our shared humanity. As a caregiver today, her lessons remain in plain sight whenever I struggle to keep an open heart.

Ralph Shapey

A completely incorrigible, cantankerous mentor of mine during graduate school at The University of Chicago. Ralph lived life according to his rules, and, while he easily made friends when he suspected that you lived your life in the same way… he as easily made many more enemies for living lives which he also suspected were something less than authentic.

A difficult man, but in a dedicated, lifelong search to manifest in his music the one ineffable quality which he held so dear… that "all great art is a miracle." As much of a character as he was, with an exceptionally colorful vocabulary, Ralph was a very spiritual man, and a great teacher who encouraged me find my authentic voice in a highly self-directed way.

Steve Jobs

Steve Jobs was another man who appeared on my radar when he was supposed to. While many write about his demanding nature, my feeling is that it reflected in a very genuine way his core beliefs and spirituality: a practicing Zen Buddhist for a large part of his life, and another influence in mine who lived it according to his own rules.

He became and remained focused on the very Zen principle of simplicity. **One of his mantras became this**: *that the most important decisions you make are not the things you do, but the things you decide not to do.* **He believed in simplicity, and in its power to change the world.** And in his own way, he did. *A mindful man who was present in the moment.*

The lives of spiritual exemplars show us an embodied spirituality *and provide us with essential criteria and clues for evaluating and explaining our own spiritual development.* Most importantly, they show us the powerful role faith can play in motivating and sustaining our efforts in the service of our most noble purpose.

How do we determine and evaluate who these people are in our lives? That has to be open to our own, very critical interpretation. These kinds of people often show up in our lives as role models who enjoy universal appeal, and with whom we very strongly connect, or want to connect.

As spiritual role models, we will typically be able to identify one core value which shines most brightly. It does so because the value is so highly integrated with their day-to-day lives, and will most probably fall into one of the following categories of authentic service: *goodness*, *noble purpose*, *success*, *integrating faith and reason*, *respect for diversity*, and *strong positive faith*.

Taking the time to look back on our lives and identify our spiritual exemplars is so much more than an exercise. It is a means by which we can begin to better understand what is of greatest value in our lives. If we don't yet possess those qualities, it is a means to that end, and it is time most well-spent. *Enjoy the process of your discovery.*

JOURNALING ASSIGNMENT 4.2

Please choose two of the exemplars presented here, or feel free to choose two of your own. Do some additional research on them, and describe each of their spiritual philosophies, and describe how you might begin to incorporate the teachings of each of them into your own life:

Name of Exemplar: _____

Philosophy: _____
_____
_____
_____

How might you incorporate the teachings of this guide into your own life?

_____
_____
_____
_____

Name of Exemplar: _____

Philosophy: _____
_____
_____
_____

How might you incorporate the teachings of this guide into your own life?

_____
_____
_____
_____

CHAPTER 5

Creating a Safe Space

SACRED SPACE
Identifying and creating a place for your spiritual centering practice.

What is a Sacred Space? *Perhaps more importantly, how can it help you?*

A Sacred Space is a safe place where you are called to go, where you can feel a distinct connection to the world around you, and also to the Divine energetic *within you.*

Sacred Space is a safe space. A special place that you feel called to... a place in which you are free to cry, to surrender, and to forgive. A place where you can re-align, re-group and re-imagine yourself, **on purpose...** as an evolving, growing, sacred being.

In this space, you are safe, and free to feel Divine love enter your heart as you let go of the pent-up anger, disappointments, and wrong steps you've taken, whether those have compromised you today, yesterday, or over the course of your entire life.

Sacred Space, *yours...* is found. It is a gift that you will come to know by the feelings of peace which it brings you. A sacred-most cathedral that, once found, will evolve as your heart's own creation; a place in which to remember and celebrate both the uniquely creative gift that you are, and also the gift of life which you have been given, wrapped not with bows or ribbons, but cocooned in the gentle glow of the ineffable, spun silk of Spirit.

Where Is It?

Start by taking the time to be mindful, noticing where your heart calls you to go, or what your heart calls you to do when you are feeling alone, disconnected from life and from others or have a need for intimate time with, and guidance from Source consciousness.

Where is that place? That place where you are called to go? Is it inside? Is it outside, in the peace and calm of nature? It can, of course, be both and that is actually good practice. It begins to introduce you to a greater stage, where you can increasingly see that the world is full of sacred spaces, all of which are capable of offering you a sense of reverence, and for your life.

What Does It Need to Be For You?

Depending on your personal needs and commitments, your Sacred Space can serve many purposes. It can be:

- Your private sanctuary, for quiet reflection, meditation, writing, painting, singing, dancing, or prayer.
- A place for making meaningful connections with others.
- A place where you can promote intimate family time, shared in reflection.
- A place that you can bring to mind from anywhere you are and find peace in that moment.

These are only a few possible objectives for creating your Sacred Space, and in each of these cases above, they can be manifested indoors, or in the great outdoors.

To What In My Life Could I Begin To Give Thought In This Space?

Any number of things. Some can of course be seasonal or more irregular in nature, but a very good case can be made for dedicating some time... even 10 - 15 minutes a day, *every day* to start, to centering within your Sacred Space:

- To celebrate a success
- To mourn a loss
- To take a pending decision or important life event into discernment
- To focus on being more present to various aspects of your life

Is It Okay To Bring Things Into My Sacred Space?

Of course. Even a single object can increase your awareness of your spirituality, enhance your connection with what is sacred to you.

This is *your* personal space, so give some thought to those things which support your focus, serenity, and potential for clarity while you're there. Things which speak to you, inspire you, and make you feel connected to a greater whole than you might find in the balance of your daily routine.

so you're made from detritus. [from exploded STARS] get over it. Or better yet, celebrate it.

AFTER ALL, what NOBLER thought can one CHERISH

THAN THAT the universe lives within us all?

- Neil deGrasse Tyson

Indoors, any number of things may make sense for you, and have some advantage in that they are protected from the elements:

- Sacred texts, poems, literature that you love, or which you want to investigate
- Music... something to make it with, or something to which to listen
- Photos or artwork
- Symbols of peace or safety, statuary
- Found objects that hold memories for you
- Candles, incense or other fragrances
- Other living things: plants, flowers, anything which reminds you that you are connected to something greater.

Outdoors, think about that which you can **bring** to the space. It could be any of the items suggested above but laid out in this case in your backpack... *an 'altar to go,' so to speak!* What is perhaps most special about this alternative is the space itself. The natural beauty of it. Its ambience. Its seclusion. Its energy. The way in which the sun kisses the trees, or the way in which the wind makes the leaves in the trees rustle.

You Know Intuitively What These Spaces Want and Need to Be

Take your Sacred Spaces as a big hug from the Spirit that already lives inside you, with which we can often lose touch. Let it be a tool that helps remind you of your innate spiritual nature. You'll be surprised how quickly you will be able to re-align with that, with your continued and regular practice.

So, honor that as you make these spaces yours. **Comfortable. Inspirational.** Whether the focus of your practice within these spaces is for daily reflection, meditation, ritual (such as yoga or other holistic practices), or ceremonies which celebrate life and your connection to it... make it a gift to your heart.

JOURNALING ASSIGNMENT 5.1

Tell us about your Sacred Space in as much detail as you can. *As with all of your Journaling Assignments, we hold what you have to say in sacred trust.*

CHAPTER 6

The Building Blocks of Spiritual Language

YOUR SPIRITUAL ALPHABET
Building blocks that embrace the energy of spiritual language in your life.

Transforming ourselves in any dimension of our being begins with a highly motivated desire to do so. In order to accomplish this goal, it will help greatly to re-evaluate our daily vocabulary, which can then help us change the landscape of our thoughts and actions, propelled by new words which we recognize as special, and which represent higher order thinking.

Read through these. The list, while by no means exhaustive, is a good point of departure. Some of them may resonate with you more than others. You will want to take those into discernment and determine what you might try changing in your daily routine as a reflection of each of them.

Bringing more and more of this highly energetic vocabulary into your personal use will almost always change your world view in ways that you may never have imagined.

In order to accomplish this spiritual transformation, we need to put the words we resonate with most into practice. Practice starts with your awareness, and often suggests how you might put each into action throughout your day.

On your first read-through, allow at least 30 minutes, making a small mark next to any of these words to which you are particularly attracted.

Attention

Pay attention, on purpose. Remove multi-tasking from your vocabulary for the moment. Notice what is going on around you, one thing at a time. **Do** one thing at a time. You are bombarded with information, often to the point of overload. Take that out of the equation and begin to notice the simplest of things. Discern how this practice changes your stress and energy levels.

Awareness

Awareness is the waking state of being consciously present. The practice of spiritual awareness begins with you, and how you perceive yourself as part of a larger whole. Once we have this view, life becomes richer, larger, and more colorful. We see connections in diversity. We treasure what we love more, as we learn of the love of others, and how it is uniquely expressed by all sentient beings. This practice brings the concept of wonder into our lives, often with the side benefit of improved emotional health. We become less subject to depression, addiction, and lethargy because we are just too busy enjoying the wonder of it all.

Beauty

Bring beauty into mind. How does it manifest within you? All around you? How does it make you feel? How do you want to act in response to it? Simplify. Enjoy the beauty of that simplicity, where each thing around you is something that you can really **see**. Take some routine out of your life. Observe how you begin to see things differently. Notice that beauty is all around you, if it can only be seen.

Be Present

There is only one moment that matters. **This** one. It's the only one you need, and honestly … it's the only one you **have**, so **be here, now**.

Are you fully aware in this moment, now? To do this successfully, you may need to let go of a few things. Regrets, missed opportunities, bad relationships, lost jobs... all kinds of things that only lead you away from being present in this moment. The future as well is not guaranteed. Thinking about what could be or what might come leads us down the same imaginary path instead of the real one on which we find ourselves right now. In this moment, right now, can you find something for which to express gratitude? Contentment? That feeling that "I am enough?"

Caring

It can be said that caring is one of the highest forms of loving. Spiritual, physical, mental, and emotional self-care allows us to love in this most extraordinary way. Where the needs of the other are allowed to outweigh the needs of the one, because we are enjoying good spiritual health. As with many other practices outlined here, the practice of caring needs to begin with you. Once we are in good spiritual health, then we can begin to extend the practice to others... family, loved ones, acquaintances, all sapient life, and, of course, the planet.

Compassion

Think for a moment beyond yourself. This can be difficult when we ourselves are suffering. When someone or something has hurt us, and we feel only a sense of lack and emptiness in our lives. And yet it is in those moments when we can begin to practice compassion. In knowing that others suffer as well, perhaps even more than we do. Give a friend, family member, loved one... even a stranger... your ear. You will change their lives for the better. Most of all, begin to have compassion for yourself. Take hurt and judgment out of the picture.

Connection

In a spiritual life, we see with every day that passes that we are deeply connected with everything on the planet. Science increasingly has come to the same conclusion. Have you eaten today? Try to trace that food all the way back to its origins, and the network of life that has touched it on its way to you. You'll be amazed. We tend to compartmentalize our lives. It's easy to tuck our experiences away and attach labels to each of them. But there is always a bigger picture. Each is part of a bigger whole. Could this be a valuable spiritual practice for you?

Devotion

Are there things in your life that you believe are inextricably connected to a Divine source? For which there is no other possible explanation? Things or events for which you feel compelled to give thanks? A devotional practice can help you keep those thoughts and feelings alive and present in you. Is self-discipline or commitment an issue in your life? A regular devotional practice may change that for you.

Dignity

The practice of dignity allows us to recognize that we are worthy of respect and cultivate a sense of pride in who we are, what we do, and what our true path is in life. With that, we can then begin to express to and reinforce in others that their lives deserve respect as well. In what ways can you begin to devote your time and energy to this vital practice? It can begin with taking a self-inventory. Do you believe that you are worthy of respect? If not, what is keeping you from the dignity that you deserve?

Enthusiasm

This moment is all there is. Are you good with it? Do you have a passion for it? Then celebrate it! If you are feeling low on energy, always tired, bored, is there something that can change that for you right now? Something to take you out of what may be nothing more than a rut you've dug yourself into? Think about it.

Empathy

The practice of empathy improves your ability to understand other's perspectives from their perspective, in a non-judgmental way. Putting yourself "in their shoes," and feeling what they are feeling. Our culture, the pace at which we live, and the time and energy demands placed on many of us can often be at odds with living a more empathic life. However, when we pause to reflect on it for a moment, it becomes clear that we all want to be heard. It is a fundamental need. In what ways might you begin practicing empathy in your life?

Equanimity

Take a look at your life with a longer view by practicing equanimity. Acknowledge that there probably have been, and that there will probably continue to be ups and downs in it. Do your best through this practice to create a more even balance, trusting that over the long haul, there is a vast middle ground of what you can call "normal." This will help take the edges off and allow you to focus on your stability in the face of uncertainty, and the inevitable storms of life. Pass it on. It is a wonderful example of spiritual activism in real life and will help you grow your empathic perspective.

Faith

There is another dimension to life. One that may be beyond our ability to experience directly, but it is there, and it brings all of life together in unity. Faith is having a relationship… the biggest, most mysterious of your life…with that. It means practicing a world view that is built on eyes that see, ears that not only hear, but listen, and a heart that is open to giving and receiving love. Does that describe you?

Forgiveness

Forgiveness is sometimes difficult for us to give. But if we think about it, it can be a major cause of our suffering. When we hold on to hurt, anger, mistrust, we live in a lower, often highly destructive energy. In forgiveness, that is released. Think about forgiveness and consider if you have work to do in that regard. **Start with you**. Are there things for which you need to forgive yourself? Then move on to others, whether they are still in your life or not. Whether they are still on this planet or not.

Grace

Grace is easier than it might seem. At its core is acceptance. Yours. Accept that you are accepted, just as you are. It is a letting go. It is simply living with an open heart—one that is willing to receive, for no good reason. Shame can sometimes get in the way of our ability to receive. Give that away.

Gratitude

The spiritual practice of gratitude is both a state of mind and a way of life. *In what ways are you, or have you been blessed?* As the saying goes, count them and say thanks. Ask yourself this, and give it some thought: "Do I have enough?" *If the answer is no,* can you truly be grateful for what you **do** have? Could your ego be getting in your own way here?

Hope

Hope allows us to dream. Our expression of it can give others hope as well. It is a powerful emotional tool and spiritual practice. Are you patient enough to have it? Looking back, when things haven't gone as planned, were you able to hold onto it? Optimists have an innate ability to "hold on while letting go." Holding on to their hope, while letting go of outcomes as they may have envisioned them.

Honesty

We all have opinions. We all make mistakes. And, if you were to research the original meaning of the word "sin," you'd soon find that all that it meant was "to miss the mark." Honesty means standing up with truth as an unbreakable value in your life. Said another way, it means being self-authentic. Once we have that concept in hand as a spiritual practice, we can then be authentic with others. Not judgmental. Honest. Able to listen with an open heart.

SILENCE is the voice of **presence.**

Listen with your HEART, **faith** is found there.

- Constance McClain

Hospitality

Living life with an open heart, capable of giving with no expectations in return. An attitude of inclusiveness, rather than exclusion. An embrace of "we," rather than one of "we and they." This can be difficult in this increasingly frenetic, often untrusting world... one where we live our lives filled with dogma that does not serve us well. Hospitality asks that we celebrate diversity, while understanding unity.

Humility

Humility asks that we find balance in our lives. To recognize that, while we should be proud of our accomplishments, we need to remain mindful that while we are unique creations of spirit, we are only one part of a vast mosaic of life, deserving respect, living our lives with dignity but no edge in our importance in the grand scheme of things. And so, in this practice, we begin to learn how to walk lightly upon the Earth. "Humility" and "Human" both come from the word "humus," or Earth. With humility, we accept our place as one among many others. Is this a practice you would find easy to adopt?

Imagination

Imagination gives juice to life. It takes us beyond the known, into a world of our own making. It is a manifestation of the infinitely, constantly creative Divine in each of us. Imagination is not an expression of the imaginary. It is the fuel for a reality of your own design. It can be a valid spiritual practice in search of your personal path, one which may transcend logic and analytical thought. It can expand our constructs of reality, and lead to a richer, more colorful life. Don't reason it away!

Integrity

Having integrity means making a mindful choice to walk the Earth as your highest self. It is a symbol of a mindful life, sourced in honesty, with all of its emotional and spiritual dimensions in consistent alignment. It is the picture of good spiritual health. It is easy for life to lead us off of our own true path, but with mindful living, we can maintain our integrity within ourselves, and with others. It is easy to see within our culture, and in the world at large, that good people can do bad things, in return for a perceived gain in their lives. Integrity through these kinds of temptations is not for the faint of heart. Do you believe that integrity is a consistent practice in your life? Do you walk the walk?

Joy

Joy is truly an out-picturing of other essential spiritual practices, namely faith, grace, gratitude, hope, and love. It is our expression of this beauty for all to see. It is a celebration of our choice to be delighted with life. It is also one of life's yin/yang springboards, such as happy/sad, or nature's own light/dark where the experience of one intensifies our awareness of the other. Do you see, and have you given thought to the importance of these kinds of opposites in your life?

Justice

Where justice is served, we will find moral, ethical, and spiritual imperatives embedded there. Justice is a common thread within the teachings of all the world's great wisdom paths. Right relationships with ourselves and with others are the building blocks of just, right living. We begin as always with ourselves, and with our increased spiritual engagement, expand that practice to all sentient beings in the interest of fair treatment for all. Justice is not a given. It is yours to demand, with respect always, to the rights and opinions of others.

Kindness

We hear a lot these days about "random acts of kindness." If you study this, you'll soon find that the acts themselves are always far from random. They are well-considered, and mindful acts of kindness that from an external perspective **appear** random. Size does not matter with them. Only that their reason for being represents the greater good, with nothing expected in return. As provincial as it can sound today, everything from good manners, to patience, to lending a small, but helping hand to someone in need. As always, it begins with our own self-awareness.

Listening

Few things can be as comforting and as validating to another as their hearing the words "I hear you" or "I see you." It demonstrates that we are **present** in the moment to others who may have a need to be heard, and that we are receptive and understanding of their suffering. We all want this to be true in our lives. It is truly a spiritual **practice**. It demands that we are present to one stream of thought in the moment, and able to filter out all of the noise in deference to that. And it demands that we listen with the intent to **hear**, not to respond.

Love

If there could be one spiritual practice that could overshadow any other, it just might be love. It is an unabashed admission that in this moment, this one and only present moment... your heart is open, and spiritually healthy. It feeds upon itself. And the opportunities that present themselves to love, to fall in love, over and over again are almost endless. It is an expression of our unity with all of life, and it begins, as with so many spiritual practices, with you. It begins with knowing that you are perfect, whole and complete just as you are, and that loving must be a two-way street. Love may change us. Love may hurt us. But when we express love, without expectation, it is life-changing.

Meaning

Meaning is an absolute cornerstone of a spiritual life. What is our life about? How do I fit in? What am I meant to do, to contribute, to give, to receive? We seek understanding from the wisdom teachers of the world, and from those who we respect, and from those who we sometimes seek approval. Take a look at the world as, just for a brief moment, an outsider. Does society provide your life with meaning? Or do your thoughts, your actions? In other words, do you believe that your life has purpose? The answer often lies in simply being you.

Non-Judgment

Do you listen with an open mind? Or do you find that you have opinions on just about everything that color the way you are able to hear? If so, you are most certainly not alone! Which is why the practice of non-judgment begins with opening your heart, which leads to opening up your mind. We begin to show compassion, and we begin to know humility. This practice is life-changing.

Nurturing

You are a unique expression of spirit. Different than anyone else on the planet. Take good care of you as there will never be another. Never let go of the exploration of why this is true. It is our self-support system, and this care promotes the growth that allows us to be in selfless service to others, and to the planet on which we live. When we are born, life centers on **receiving** nourishment. Our choice in subsequent years is to learn to give it as well. The key to success here is often knowing balance in our lives. If we do not acknowledge the importance of receiving, we become less capable to give. Are you in balance?

Openness

It is difficult for many of us to remain open, on a number of levels. Open to new ideas, open to ideologies other than our own, open to possibility, open in our hearts. It demands an empathy towards others, and a willingness to receive that the universe, not us, is often in control. It asks that we go with the flow, that we sidestep judging. It is easy to become rigid, and subject to dogma. Are you approachable to others? Do you have preconceived notions about outcomes of situations in your life? Are you open to new thinking, new experience?

Peace

Peace is not just turned on or off. It is promoted, step-by-step, in the interest of the unity that is inherent on our planet. Step-by-step, we grow. Peace grows, and is a common goal of all spiritual practices. It manifests as inner well-being, and also as your ability to promote that well-being into the world. The ancient wisdom path of Judaism underscores this important duality. "Shalom," the root word for peace, means whole... whole within oneself, and between the peoples of the world. Can you disarm yourself in this world of firearms as a right? Do you believe that it can help to disarm the world?

Play

Play is a willingness to express ourselves, our emotions, our joy... with abandon. It is incredibly important to our self-care, and in our relationships with others. It expresses our joy, our wonder, and helps to keep our search for meaning real. It is often best expressed in our willingness to be spontaneous. To live in the moment. To smile. To laugh. To express our feelings in a light hearted way. Responsibilities in life can run the risk of dampening our ability to play. Is that true in your life?

Questing

What is a quest? It is a journey. One that can serve to deepen your faith from a heart-centered level. It asks that we go into what for us is the unknown and learn. It is not about conquering. It is not about winning. It is about healing, and about answering questions that need to be answered. Questing means traveling somewhere with which you have no familiarity. That can mean physically. It can also mean psychologically. It is an adventure. It is also a surrender to that which you think you know. It is a means to spiritual healing. Do you feel that you need a quest in your life?

Reverence

Consider practicing reverence for life. All of it. Consider that the sacred is within all sentient beings, uniquely expressed, on the planet. Treat it all with the respect and awe that you yourself deserve. Treat it all as parts of one magnificent creation. No living thing on this planet is beneath reverence. Keep alive the wonder of that. Keep alive the well-deserved self-esteem that we all should feel as shepherds of this magnificent creation... all of us collected on one big living rock on which we all deserve to co-exist.

Shadow

We hope to live in the light. And with that light, shadow is cast. This shadow exists in each of our lives as our imperfections. Our demons. They have something to say. We need to listen and accept them in their own context. The anger we hold on to, the jealousy we feel, the hurt we have done. All that of which we are not proud, but which still exist. This critical spiritual practice allows us to embrace the light and the shadow as the only way in which we can fully embrace our humanity. Take a few moments to discern whether or not you are projecting your shadow onto others.

Silence

Silence is a difficult commodity to acquire in today's world. Finding that place where it can exist for you can often be a daunting challenge. Where there is no media of any kind playing. None. A place where your inner sanctuary lives. That place where spirit lives. That place where you can withdraw from the world, if only for a precious moment.

Teachers

Embrace learning. Embrace that there is something to learn... always. The teachers may be very different from you, and from your prevailing outlook on life. They are, and can be with your participation, a part of your spiritual unfolding in this life. They may instruct through stories or personal example. They may instruct through readings. They may instruct through the experiential. But they will all exist for only one reason: to challenge you forward in your spiritual quest.

Transformation

Breathe. Your spiritual wholeness and healing await. Spiritual practice embraces the personal deepening that takes place when we get in touch with our oneness with source.

This, often, is also an embrace of the new, that which is outside of our patterns, our habits... the dogma by which we have chosen to live. This change is not a simple one. It asks us to take deep issues into discernment. It asks that we admit change into our lives. Do you embrace change?

Unity

In this age of global spirituality, time has come to respect differences, while we accept commonalities... working together with those who are trying to make the world a better place. This can be as simple as acknowledging how alike you are with others. We can come to believe that we need to be very protective of our turf and highly individualistic... only interested in having our own way, especially in a fast-paced environment. It extends beyond the people in our life, however. Consider your concept of unity with the entire planet.

Vision

You have a personal vision. It is your world view. It is no less important than anyone else's. But it is unique, as you are. Use the wisdom of your own personal visions to renew yourself, and to renew your community. Vision is a spiritual practice that encompasses the discovery of fresh insights about the way things are, and outlooks on the way they can be. Vision, taking a moment apart from what is, can give you a more balanced, forward-thinking outlook on life.

Wonder

Celebrate the rich, amazing diversity of life—yours, and all of the life in its abundance around you, interconnected with you. Your own curiosity will lead you, again and again, to wonders big and small, without end. This is **your** life, and your **adventure** to enjoy. Bring all of you to the party... all of your senses, in mindful play. Notice as you begin this practice your level of engagement with life, and with yourself.

The X - Factor

Embrace the unknown. Observe and bask in the rich diversity of life... how you, and each sentient being you encounter is a completely unique expression of spirit. There is no reason to press for answers why it is so. It is beyond our ability to know. Only that we respect the mystery, wrapped as we are, as the ancient mystics would say, in this cloud of unknowing. We do not need to have all the answers, nor do we need to try to reduce the complexities of our lives into sound bytes and video clips. Take relish in the inexplicability of life, with the wide-eyed wonder of a beginner's mind.

Yearning

Yearning grows through our spiritual practices as an increasing desire to know completeness. Our need to know that there is something more than that which our senses might show us. It is our attraction to the unity of all life. To our presence in each other, in every living thing. Reach for more. It is there. Believe in its possibility. Yearning is a powerful spiritual and emotional practice, one which mystics have embraced for millenia, in their quest to better know the love that has created us all.

You

You are a unique expression of spirit. Your life moves forward moment by ever-present moment as a co-creator of all of life in its infinite dimension. The stuff of the universe is within you. And so, you are important. You are in service, the service of becoming your very best you. Being you demands our acceptance of ourselves. All of you... the good and the bad. The practice of you is to remember balance. Be proud and be humble as well. Be assertive, and flexible as well. Be you, in balance with yourself and with all of the life around you. You are much more than you may believe yourself to be.

Zeal/Zest

Zeal is our passion for life, and the passion that life arouses in us. The more that we begin to connect with the life all around us, the more we become energized by it. With it, we can know gratitude for who we are, and what, in its abundance, we have been given. With it, we can show compassion for all living beings. This is a fundamental energy, and a key spiritual practice. In our ability to receive, we are enriched. It allows us to live, rather than know only an unlived life, as we watch it pass us by. Are you in? If not, what do you feel is holding you back?

JOURNALING ASSIGNMENT 6.1

Now review the words you have marked, and again, choose your top ten, and give us your reasoning for having chosen each one. *Is it already a part of your personal spiritual alphabet? Why? Is it a quality to which you aspire? If so, why?*

My Top 10 Qualities - Ranked *(1 = most important, 10 = least)*

#1 _____

I chose this quality because: _____

_____

_____

_____

#2 _____

I chose this quality because: _____

_____

_____

_____

#3 _____

I chose this quality because: _____

_____

_____

_____

#4 _____

I chose this quality because: _____

_____

_____

_____

#5 _____

I chose this quality because: _____

_____

_____

_____

#6   _____

I chose this quality because: _____

_____

_____

_____

#7   _____

I chose this quality because: _____

_____

_____

_____

#8   _____

I chose this quality because: _____

_____

_____

_____

#9   _____

I chose this quality because: _____

_____

_____

_____

#10 _____

I chose this quality because: _____

_____

_____

_____

Words are the building blocks by which we express our thoughts, and thoughts become things.
It's worth spending time on the ones which frame our thoughts in a really central way.

The only thing REAL about your **journey** is the STEP you are taking at this **moment**.

That's all there ever is.

– Eckhart Tolle

48 HOUR PRESENCE
Assessing your awareness in a chaotic world.

Let's begin with a quick reflection.

> *Where have you been over the past forty-eight hours?*
> *How many of your thoughts can you remember?*
> *How many actions did you take, and what were they?*
> *Who were you with?*
> *What did you talk about?*

Too difficult to remember? *If so, then we'd like to invite you to your next challenge*: **the 48 Hour Presence.**

The **48 Hour Presence** exercise is an outgrowth of your work with the **Spiritual Alphabet** where you identified ten spiritual words which spoke to you because they resonated with your core values, and which also might have represented areas in which you felt you needed to grow. For either of these reasons, these were the words that most stood out to you. In the moment, it didn't really matter why you chose them… just that you chose them and *we'd examine the 'why' later.*

The Spiritual Alphabet exercise began the process for you of looking *inward* at the ways in which you look *out upon* the world, giving you a deeper awareness of your ***unique spiritual lens…*** that filter through which you see the world, every day.

JOURNALING ASSIGNMENT 6.2

Now, ***let's narrow that list down to your top three words***. This might be a challenge for you, as you begin to discern ever more carefully what makes up, or what is missing from the spiritual lens through which you currently see the world. ***But as you take this into discernment now,*** *we believe that you'll begin to realize just how important each one is to your well-being.*

What are your top three, in no particular order of importance?

_____

_____

_____

Next, one more challenge. *Narrow your new list of three spiritual qualities down to one.* **One word, one quality you'd most like to embellish within your core.** *One more time, this time doing your best to discern the one spiritual quality most important to you right now, in this moment of your life.*

Which spiritual quality do you think will *benefit you and those people around you the most*, whether family, friends, co-workers, or even complete strangers? ***List it here:***

_____

Great. *Now that you've determined your number one choice* (don't worry, this experience can, and should be repeated as the months and years go by), you're ready to start the 48 Hour Presence experience, *which is going to ask a heightened level of conscious awareness, concentration and attention of you.*

The goal of the exercise is for you to observe yourself: your thoughts, your actions, and your interactions with others with respect to the word you've chosen.

As an example:

Trevor has chosen ***patience*** for his 48 Hour Presence experiment. He has chosen Patience because he tends to be impatient almost all the time, with almost everything, and he has realized his impatience often leads to a number of behaviors and outcomes with which he's not happy.

He often cuts people off on the freeway that are driving too slow for him, regardless of the speed limit.

He also interrupts other people when they are trying to have a conversation with him. He does this because he's not really listening to them in the first place, because he believes that his opinion is the only one that really matters.

Trevor's (and your) objective afterwards is to write how this quality, good or bad affects his life, and what he (you) might do to make for better outcomes.

So, to start, once you've focused solely on the word you've chosen… for example: peace, ineffability, hospitality, love, kindness, generosity *(refer back to the Spiritual Alphabet for the entire list)*… the next step is to self-assess your ability to stay as fully present with this experiment as you can.

This is a 48 hour commitment.

Going in, on a scale of 1-10 (with 10 being that you believe you can stay spiritually focused on this for two days, two nights), what do you assess as your chances of success? Write that down, and make sure to include that initial observation along with your final report.

Of course, everyone's schedule is very different from the next person's, so you'll need to determine what the best start and stop times are for this exercise.

We'll just throw it out there that, based on years of collecting data on this, we've found that the experience works best for most people when it starts upon waking up on a Wednesday or Thursday morning, and finishes up at the roughly the same time on a Saturday morning.

Why? Because it comes towards the end of a week, when early on stresses are behind you, and finishes before the weekend comes into play… so often a period where the list of errands is long, and available time is precious. *That being said, it's up to you to choose the most optimal time to begin.*

Go ahead, and best of luck!

JOURNALING ASSIGNMENT 6.3

Once you have successfully completed this exercise, please share your thoughts, and answer these questions as honestly as possible. *Knowing our motivations for our behaviors can actually strengthen the experience for us.*

How easy or difficult was this experience? *(place a mark on the continuum below)*

extremely difficult

moderately challenging

5

easy

1

10

List all the insights you recognized during this experience. *About the way this word affects the way you see (and interact with) yourself, your friends, loved ones, associates at work, and even complete strangers.*

_____

_____

_____

_____

_____

_____

_____

_____

_____

_____

How has this experience changed (transformed) you?

_____

_____

_____

_____

_____

_____

_____

_____

_____

_____

If you plan on repeating this experience with another quality or two, which ones will you choose? *Why?*

_____

_____

_____

_____

_____

_____

_____

_____

_____

_____

CHAPTER 7
Cultivating Our Presence in the World

THE GRACE OF GRATITUDE
A transformative spiritual practice.

Gratitude is a quality we can feel when we are *thankful* for something another has done on our behalf.

It's also an attitude that we can choose to more fully, continuously embody.

One way to make this concept manifest is by making a spiritual decision to begin each day with a short gratitude practice. So, find a blank journal. *The size, and whether or not it is lined is your choice.*

Once you're fully awake, take three to five minutes to sit down in a quiet place. Close your eyes gently, relax your breathing, and ask yourself two questions:

"What am I truly grateful for?
"Who am I deeply grateful for having, or having had in my life?

See how it goes.

A second, great time to journal is just before going to bed. Try taking a few minutes to review the day, specifically looking for all the big and small experiences you lived for which you now realize you are grateful. Before long, you might begin seeing a picture of your life that you may not have been able to see before starting this practice, wrapped now in an "attitude of gratitude."

It can be an amazingly *transformative practice* when we take the time to really recognize all that we are deeply grateful for in our lives. When we are able to see, even with our daily struggles… *how fortunate we are.*

It's easy to let life, and all that it sometimes hands us *program us with self-defeating narratives that can so often hijack our highest self.*

Journaling is a great way to keep that chatter to a minimum, and living **an intentional, spiritually engaged life is just a much lighter load for all of us to carry.**

THE SELFISH PHENOMENON OF TAKING THINGS FOR GRANTED

Working on our ability to give thanks in good times and bad.

It's easy to give thanks in times of joy and happiness. Not so much during times of stress and crisis. Take this opportunity to write down a list of a dozen things for which you are grateful. *Some of them may actually stem from things you often take for granted.*

JOURNALING ASSIGNMENT 7.1

_____

_____

_____

_____

_____

_____

_____

_____

Please take a few moments now to reflect on any feelings that may have arisen as you took this gratitude inventory.

_____

_____

_____

_____

_____

_____

_____

Wherever you go, there you are.

- Zen teaching

HOW OFTEN ARE WE REALLY HERE?
Benefits of quieting the mind, setting intentions, and being present in the moment.

Do you ever catch yourself daydreaming? Our wild guess would be yes. But what can be a much more telling observation is how often, and how unconsciously we do it. *Paying attention is not as straight forward as we might think it is.* If we are being honest, we have to admit that we are a seriously distracted society, in a world populated by technologies designed to distract us in millions of different ways and means.

We have the ability, if we have the money… to wear our window to the world on our sleeves. The computing ability and technological advances inside of our cell phones dwarf the capabilities of the computers that put us on the moon.

Incredible advances, not even imagined a hundred years ago. But at what cost? **Consider for a moment how much information is out there:**

Our global Internet population now exceeds 4 billion humans. On average, in the US alone **we produce close to 3,000,000 gigabytes of Internet data every minute, including:**

- Over 15 million texts a minute.
- Over 450,000 tweets a minute.
- Over 40,000 Instagram posts a minute.
- Over 3.5 million Google searches a minute.
- Over 100 million spam emails a minute.

We live in a world where data never sleeps. We forget that **we**, on the other hand, need our downtime. We need it in order to be fully present to the importance of the moment. Without it, we become present to nothing, in a vain attempt to be present to everything.

We need space and time to simply being instead of constantly doing. As its been said by many folks in many different ways, we are *not* born to live lives of non-stop doing… we are meant to be Human Beings, *something far different than Human Doings.*

So in this moment now, *let's take the time to step outside of ourselves,* so that we can better *observe* ourselves. **Please read and re-read the following passage for the next five minutes.** *Observe yourself.* **Take notes,** *objectively* as to where your mind actually is during this time, and **try to remember as much about the content as possible:**

> *"Tom's most well now and got his bullet around his neck on a watch-guard for a watch, and is always seeing what time it is, and so there ain't nothing more to write about, and I am rotten glad of it, because if I'd a knowed what a trouble it was to make a book I wouldn't a tackled it, and ain't a-going to no more. But I reckon I got to light out for the Territory ahead of the rest, because Aunt Sally she's going to adopt me and sivilize me, and I can't stand it. I been there before."*
>
> -Mark Twain
> *Adventures of Huckleberry Finn*

JOURNALING ASSIGNMENT 7.2

Please take a few moments to answer the following questions (we're on the honor system here!):

Without looking back at the material you just read, from what book is this excerpt?

_____
_____
_____

Who is the author of the book?

_____
_____
_____

Huck Finn is the character who is speaking in this excerpt. Who was he talking about at the beginning of the passage?

_____
_____
_____

What was Tom wearing in order to tell time?

_____

_____

_____

Where is Huck Finn headed?

_____

_____

_____

Before you started this exercise, you may have believed that your focus would be, and would remain on reading... _but was it?_ Can you honestly say that your concentration remained on the paragraph above, or did you find that, here and there you were "losing your mind"?

Another possibility, _which is harder to hear_ **is that you were completely unaware** of the never-ending array of _mindless thoughts_ that were running through your mind _that kept your focus everywhere but on the material at hand?_

Any degree of this distraction is common for many of us, and is often described, all over the world as "monkey mind," our inability to quiet the many thoughts, the chatter, that we often experience in our heads. As common as it is, though, distraction clearly lowers retention.

So, what can we do about it? **It's easy to become distracted.** You may notice it most when you're trying to study, or when you're trying to focus when working on a project that demands your full concentration. So many thoughts can get in our way that our heads can feel like they are hosting a World Championship Ping Pong tournament! **Paying attention** can be difficult for many of us, but there are ways to improve… and in the process, increase our ability to attend to one task at a time.

Paying attention begins with setting intention.

Attention may also be understood as our giving **full presence** to the moment. As we continue our studies, it will become increasingly clear that our presence, consistently... is critical to steering our life choices in more spiritually healthy directions.

A helpful first step in improving our capacity for attention, our ability to be present, *is setting our intention for the moment.*

When we set an intention to accomplish something, we add a significant power to achievement of that goal, and as a proven, practical strategy, scientific study has shown that this practice can have huge benefits:

> "Deciding in advance when and where you will take specific actions
> to reach your goal *can double or triple your chances for success!*"

-Heidi Grant Halvorson,
Associate Director of the Motivation Science Center
Columbia Business School

CHAPTER 8
Balance, Presence, and Change

THE THOUGHT CONTINUUM
And the dangers of past/future thinking.

Since the beginning of time, human beings have had to navigate what we call the Thought Continuum. It addresses our tendency to *project into the future and ruminate on the past,* rather than cultivating our ability to be present in the moment.

These projections (also referred to as expectations) and ruminations (usually tied up in past disappointments of both real and often perceived betrayals), *can set up a pattern of thinking that is unhelpful for most of us.* Here's why:

ruminations (the past)	**THE PRESENT MOMENT**	expectations (the future)

Expectations

We all hope, wish, and plan for specific results in our lives. That is natural. In the process, however, we often lose sight of the fact that life is far larger than we are personally able to control. When life inserts itself into the mix, it can often affect our plans radically, often in ways that fall short of our projections, bringing only disappointment, and a sense of failure. And while it's often completely outside of our control, we find ourselves on an emotional roller coaster, where along the ride, we have feelings of regret, sadness, and even clinical depression.

Rumination

When we ruminate, it's all too easy to get caught up in cycles of anger, despair, and loss of self-worth. As with living with future expectations, ruminating on the past can become an even more unhealthy, vicious cycle to anyone caught in its power. *Its fundamental energy is one of loss.* Of things, people, feelings that are lost forever. This kind of negative energy can easily have a life all its own, and, just like a small bug caught in a spider's web, breaking free can be impossible without help.

*Let's take a closer look at how our expectations and ruminations can hijack our **nows**.* **A hijacked brain is an actual neurobiological experience.** *Stressful events in our lives effect two key areas of our brain: the hippocampus (a part of the limbic system, which regulates emotions), and the amygdala (responsible for survival instincts, and memory).*

So, we typically experience stress **emotionally** (our emotions are running amok and our memory centers are thrown off), which can often escalate our stress response well beyond the actual scope of the situation... and we forget simple things... like where we put our keys, or phones. *This is the concept of a brain hijacked under stress.*

JOURNALING ASSIGNMENT 8.1

Try to remember a time recently when you were incapable of making a clear decision. Chances are that you can, and that, in that moment... *you may have been in a hijacked state of mind.*

What caused the hijack? Can you recall the situation? If it was a stressful one, can you describe it, and why it was stressful? What were you feeling? How was your body reacting? How, if at all, did your behavior change? What tools, if any, did you have at your disposal to deal with the situation? If none, is this something that you want to change in your life?

Take a few moments to journal this:

_____

_____

_____

_____

_____

_____

_____

_____

_____

_____

_____

EQUANIMITY
When life comes into balance.

Most of us want to find a place of *inner peace* for our lives. This inner peace speaks to our ability to maintain ease within our psyche, our emotions, our thoughts and our bodies... *the complete experience of living our lives.*

When we cultivate a state of equanimity, *we gain the skills to remain calm while under pressure or stress.* Many of us lack this beautiful quality of life, for the simple reason we've never been shown how to cultivate it for ourselves.

What a shame.

How do we learn to develop a mind filled with poise, exquisite self-control, and mental clarity... *even under pressure?*

To begin, we can become conscious of what one of our favorite Buddhist teachers, Alan Wallace, PhD calls: "The Four Immeasurables," which are also associated with Metta, or Loving Kindness meditation.

With them, we can begin to become conscious of creating a strong foundation of **mental stability**. We see this beginning in yoga as well, when standing in 'tadasana,' or Mountain Pose, where we visualize a powerfully strong mountain, as we breathe with stability in mind.

the 4 immeasurables are:

Love

the wish that other beings may be happy, and that they have all the means to achieve happiness.

Compassion

the wish that other beings are free of pain and suffering, and free of all causes of pain and suffering.

Sympathetic Joy

the joy that arises in us when others experience joy and happiness, and an open-heartedness that shuts out selfishness.

Equanimity

seeing and experiencing everybody as equal, without any distortion or personal bias.

Holding The Four Immeasurables consciously in mind begins to establish for us that, underneath all of the superficial with which we distinguish one of us from another… there is something more profound that is the same in all of us. ***This is the unifying consciousness that is also referred to as non-duality.***

It is a mindful presence where we begin to fully experience life in a liberated, fearless and compassionate way, shared with all sentient beings. In a word, **mindfulness**.

The many and miraculous benefits of the ancient practice of mindfulness are profound.
Research tells us that with even only 15-20 minutes a day of any form of mindfulness training, we will begin to experience a significant life change, including:

- increased *empathy* and *equanimity*
- lowered blood pressure
- improved listening and perceptual skills
- improved mood
- improved awareness of the world within and around us.

These benefits improve our lives by enhancing our moment-by-moment reasoning skills, and shaping for ourselves an objective, more non-judgmental existence.

Mindfulness can be practiced while sitting (zazen), walking, or even while standing!

Love is a sacred reserve of energy.

It is like the blood of spiritual evolution.

- Pierre Teilhard de Chardin

With a solid mindfulness practice, we can open healthier new worlds of understanding and perception simply by practicing every day. One where, like a breath of fresh air, we begin to feel our hearts and minds expanding into worlds of inner peace, equanimity, and improved self-respect.

We hope you'll give it a try. It has been life-changing for us, and for thousands across the planet.

IMPEDIMENTS ALONG THE WAY
Roadblocks you may encounter on the path towards spiritual growth.

Barriers, impediments, and distractions are all road blocks that can pull us off of our spiritual journey - *indefinitely*. Distractions are like younger siblings or children, always grabbing for our attention, pulling us off of our path. But if we are to keep ourselves honest here, these distractions are often self-made… cell phones, social media, music, television, or addictions… and they can all too easily impede your smooth realization of a richer, deeper, more consciously aware life.

In and of themselves, none of these are inherently evil. But they can interrupt the degree of our spiritual awareness, and also hijack the commitment to our spiritual practices… so, as with everything… balance is key to maintaining a mindful presence to the energetics of our spiritual growth.

These spiritual distractions are commonly called "temptations," and classically, we have found them embedded in the literary form of the fairy tale. *Little Red Riding Hood* would be an example. *Temptations are rooted in people, things or concepts which attract us, strongly, as a magnet to metal.* If our journey is to endure, and succeed, we need to be determined to bring these distractions into balance.

Doing that first requires that we recognize what they are, so let's take an opportunity now to inventory them.

Journaling Assignment 8.2

Look carefully and compile a list of everything that regularly or sporadically distracts you from being otherwise focused. Nothing is too small, nothing too inconsequential. This is not a time to be judgmental, only truthful. The size of the list you end up with may surprise you, but that's okay. Once you are awake to all of your interruptions, you can begin to assess their importance, and make more room for the spiritual dimension in your life.

Part 1

Make your personal list here. Describe each one fully. How much time does each consume? How, and to what degree does each affect your ability to concentrate and remain focused on the present moment? **Time is a critical asset,** *and one that we really don't in fact own.* When it is lost, it is lost forever.

1. _____
   _____

2. _____
   _____

3. _____
   _____

Part 2

For each distraction you've identified, describe how you might release it, or significantly reduce your involvement with it. Rank how much time they consume on a regular basis. Rank how hard each would be to bring into better balance and allow you to become more spiritually conscious on a more consistent basis.

1. _____
   _____

2. _____
   _____

3. _____

_____

SEASONS OF THE SOUL
Examples of our InterConnectedness.

You may have come across the phrase "seasons of the soul."

If you have, it's likely that what you found was a broad reference to the process of our aging, passing through the seasons of our life. You may even have heard the reference being made in the classic song "It Was A Very Good Year," written in the 1960s by Ervin Drake, and made famous by Frank Sinatra, as a man, now growing older, reflects on the seasons of his life:

When I was seventeen, it was a very good year.
It was a very good year for small town girls and soft summer nights.
We'd hide from the lights on the village green.
When I was seventeen.

When I was twenty-one, it was a very good year.
It was a very good year for city girls who lived up the stairs.
With perfumed hair that came undone.
When I was twenty-one.

Then I was thirty-five, it was a very good year.
It was a very good year for blue-blooded girls of independent means.
We'd ride in limousines, their chauffeurs would drive.
When I was thirty-five

But now the days grow short, I'm in the autumn of the year
And now I think of my life as vintage wine from fine old kegs.
From the brim to the dregs, it poured sweet and clear.
It was a very good year.

You'll also find this type of reference in a variety of literature attributed to the world's great wisdom paths. One example where the concept is most deeply engrained comes from the Hindu tradition, which suggests that at different stages of our life, there are four things that we really want:

- Pleasure - seeking personal happiness and attending to your needs
- Success - enhancing your happiness through acquisition of wealth, Fame, and power
- Renunciation - searching for meaning and value
- Duty - helping others.

You can easily see the seasons of a life play out in this as well. When we are young, personal pleasure often can play out as a dimension of primary importance in our lives. As we age, we want to acquire things as a symbol of our success. Later on in life, we often find ourselves asking the question: "is that all there is?" And towards the end of our life, when we as elders feel it is our duty to share our experience with the next generation.

The seasons of our life *are the broadly brushed seasons of our soul.* Of course, we *physically* go through the seasons of our Mother Earth many times in our lifetime. But it is very much the same with *our soul.* Consider …

There are times when we need to be alone. To quiet the mind and listen for our highest voice… our greatest purpose. By any other name, this is soul-searching, where we unplug and go inward for our answers. *This is Autumn, our time of centering.*

There are times when we need to cleanse. To let go of anything which does not serve: people, thoughts, beliefs, and attitudes that have begun to get in our way. Once we have centered ourselves by quieting our minds, we can then begin to take inventory of what's inside and releasing whatever no longer serves. *This is the classically barren season of Winter… a time of emptying.*

There are times when we need to grow into our mind. To hear our creative voice, to listen to our intuition, and to trust our mind. This is a time to let go of ego, and connect with something higher, more personal. To prepare to simply receive, without judgment, the creativity that surrounds us, and which will feed us if we let it! Where we can experience a relaxed receptivity to the Divine in each of us. This is where we can ask ourselves the big questions, like: "Who Am I?" and "Why Am I Here?" *This is Spring… a time for grounding.*

And finally, *there are times when we need to share.* Everything that we've learned to trust, everything that we've learned to cultivate, and to bring it into community with others. To celebrate what we've learned of ourselves. To communicate who we are, what we stand for, and hopefully in the process, enrich the lives of others who we touch. ***This is Summer... a time for sharing, and a time for connecting.***

-ref. Brian Luke Seaward
"Health & The Human Spirit"

This can be an invaluable practice. It's a way to give ourselves a spiritual health checkup every now and then, when things seem to be out of balance in some way. It can also help you self-direct in your relationships with others:

> *If you're in the cleansing mode of Winter, is it a wise time to initiate, or expect success in a relationship with someone who is in Summer?*

Sharing these self-assessments with someone important in your life introduces a whole new dimension of honesty into your communications, *and it can also be a great way to build spirituality in your relationship.*

JOURNALING ASSIGNMENT 8.3

And so, in leaving this topic, a few questions for you to consider. *Please write a short paragraph describing:*

What season do you feel you're in right now? *Why?*

_____

_____

_____

_____

_____

_____

Autumn is the season of centering. *How do you do that in your life today? Is it easy for you to stay centered? If not, why do you suppose that is?*

_____

_____

_____

_____

Winter is the season of emptying. *We like to avoid this one but can remain stuck there for what can seem like an eternity! Is there something or someone in your life now which you need to let go? If so, please describe. If not, please write down your feelings about emptying. Is it hard, or easy for you? Why?*

_____

_____

_____

_____

Spring is the season of grounding. *Are you grounded? How do you achieve that? Is that an easy state to achieve after you've gone through a winter of emptying? Or does it take time for new seeds of change to grow?*

_____

_____

_____

_____

Summer is the season of connecting. *What are your "go to" ways by which you make connections… with yourself, with others, with the Earth or with Spirit?*

_____

_____

_____

_____

-ref. Brian Luke Seaward
"Health & The Human Spirit"

CHAPTER 9
Meditation and our Quest for Clarity

Do not dwell on the **past**, do not **dream** of the future, concentrate the **mind** on the PRESENT MOMENT.

- Buddha

Meditation
What Is It, and Why Do It?

These questions are reverberating around our entire planet at this point in the human experience here on Earth. The answers, the reasons why, are many, increasing, and come from scientific as well as spiritual communities all across the planet, from improving our physiology, and physical health, to improving our emotional, psychological, and spiritual health.

Meditation is first and foremost a mainstay practice in the contemplative traditions, *if not since the dawn of man, then for a very long time*. Findings suggest that prehistoric cultures and religions often practiced a kind of repetitive chanting in order to bring a focused result in thinking. This has evolved over time in a direct way to become what we know today as either **chants**, or **mantras**… still an oral tradition *(more on that in another section)*.

Some of the earliest written records of meditation come from the Hindu traditions of Vedantism, in around 1500 BCE. Much later, in around the 6th to 5th centuries BCE, other forms of meditation developed in both Taoist China and Buddhist India. **Through the centuries, meditation has become an integral part of all of the world's great wisdom paths**… Hinduism, Buddhism, Islam, Christianity, and Judaism alike, *with varying approaches to its practice, but with remarkably similar intent.*

Why have these traditions taken such deep root in human civilization?

In a nutshell, our quest for clarity. Our quest for calm. And in achieving that, an increased opportunity to live life more fully. To be present in the moment. To rid ourselves of the constant distractions which we self-present… that tendency we commonly refer to as "monkey mind."
This term came from no other than the Buddha himself, *who described the mind as being filled with drunken monkeys, jumping around, screeching, chattering, carrying on endlessly.* "We all have monkey minds," Buddha said, "with dozens of monkeys all clamoring for attention. Fear is an especially loud monkey, sounding the alarm incessantly, pointing out all the things we should be wary of and everything that could go wrong."

And so, Buddha, along with other mystics and contemplatives like Confucious and Lao Tzu, came upon the power of calming and quieting the mind.

135

Its purpose is singular. *What it is called will vary*: "Hitbodedut" in Judaism. "Muraqaba" in the Sufi tradition of Islam. "Dhyana" in both Buddhism and Hinduism (as Sanskrit is a common language to both).

In Christianity, the word became meditation, from the Latin word "Meditari," which has a range of meanings, including: to reflect on, to study, and to practice *(most commonly, reflection, and discernment)*. Christian meditation is the process of deliberately focusing on specific thoughts (such as a bible passage) and reflecting on their meaning in the context of the love of God.

In the western world, the word "meditation" has stuck with its practitioners, and in a spiritual context, it exists first and foremost as a practice to **observe** the mind, and is **not** of necessity associated with a religious path.

A good way to look at how the practice of meditation can be best approached is by first learning to authentically discern our thoughts and feelings (physical and emotional) from the outside looking in, as somewhat of a third party observer would: moment by moment, and without judgment.

This begins to offer us increased clarity of our most genuine, **true** self, by removing our mental clutter, and silencing our internal and external environments in order to better see who we really are *(which many mystics would call God)*.

We call this state of being mindfulness, and it is **Mindfulness Meditation**, with its focus on conscious awareness of the breath, which has endured today as a mainstream practice in all world cultures with tangible physical, emotional, and spiritual health benefits.

Ancient Hindu yogis found that placing focused, conscious awareness on the breath helped to crystallize the mind and could settle down the interruptive monkey mind. These calming techniques rapidly made their way to the east, where the Buddha experienced the very same result for himself. Later, around the 6th century BCE, this breath practice was integrated with the gentle, flowing movements of Qi-Gong. Over time, these same practices eventually made their way to the west.

Let's take a look at several types of meditative practice, which have endured for centuries.

VIPASSANA OR INSIGHT MEDITATION

Vipassana in the Buddhist tradition means insight into the true nature of reality, the "three marks of existence:" *impermanence, suffering,* and *the realization of the non-self…* non ego-involved presence.

Also known as "insight meditation," Vipassana focuses on being mindful of our breath, our body functions, and our thoughts, moment by moment, in order to gain insight into these three marks of existence.

This practice extends into the everyday, as a living practice: walking, washing the dishes, folding the laundry, brushing your teeth, eating, and many more day-to-day activities to which we may not otherwise pay much attention. It is this seminal Zen Buddhist concept of seeking insight which is the precursor of what we today call "mindfulness" in the western world, re-cast in large part as a spiritual practice, free of religious association.

*And now… **a few thoughts from the Dalai Lama on meditation**:*

"Generally speaking, our mind is predominantly directed towards external objects. Our attention follows after the sense experiences.

It remains at a predominantly sensory and conceptual level. In other words, normally our awareness is directed towards physical sensory experiences and mental concepts.

But in this exercise, what you should do is withdraw your mind inward; *don't let it chase after or pay attention to sensory objects.* At the same time, don't allow it to be so totally withdrawn that there is a kind of dullness or lack of mindfulness.

You should *maintain a very full state of alertness and mindfulness,* and then try to see the natural state of your consciousness — a state in which your consciousness is not afflicted by thoughts of the past, the things that have happened, your memories and remembrances; nor is it afflicted by thoughts of the future, like your future plans, anticipations, fears, and hopes. But rather, try to remain in a natural and neutral state."

How does he actually practice bringing his natural state to his awareness?

"This is a bit like a river that is flowing quite strongly, in which you cannot see the riverbed very clearly.

If, however, there was some way you could stop the flow in both directions, from where the water is coming and to where the water is flowing, then you could keep the water still.

That would allow you to see the base of the river quite clearly.

Similarly, *when you are able to stop your mind from chasing sensory objects and thinking about the past and future and so on, and when you can free your mind from being totally 'blanked out' as well, then you will begin to see underneath this turbulence* of the thought processes.

There is an underlying stillness, an underlying clarity of the mind. You should try to observe or experience this."

And that is all there is to it. **Now let's examine some variant forms of meditation.**

WALKING MINDFULNESS MEDITATION
In a mindful walking meditation, we begin in **Noble Silence**.

Noble Silence is a powerful part of any mindfulness practice. It helps us hear our inner voice, and allows us to contemplate how that inner voice affects our external reality. It honors the sanctity of the practice and shows respect for others with whom you are practicing.

As we begin our walk, our intention is focused on the walking itself, beginning with establishing a **considerably** *slower-than-usual pace* for ourselves. *With your very first few steps,* **draw full awareness inward to your body**, and to the sensations of your breath moving freely through you.

Breathe, *deeply,* at a rate which approximates the pace of your walking. Become conscious in your effort to begin to coordinate your breath with every step.

Next, **take your awareness to your legs and feet.** *Notice each step.* Feel the sensations in your feet and legs as they make contact with the ground. **If you notice your foot strike is heavy,** *see if you can lighten up a bit,* but without making any self-judgments about your weight.

Notice your posture. *Are you walking with an upright, noble posture?* Or are you slouching, burdened down with thoughts and emotions? **A walking meditation is intended to be a light, easeful experience for your body**.

As you gain comfort with this slow-paced, mindful walking meditation, *try incorporating another related practice with it*, called **"looking meditation."** *This can, of course, be done as a separate meditation*, but when integrated with your walking you will find that, as Aristotle once said:

"The whole is greater than the sum of its parts."

To bring this in, begin by letting your attention be pulled to your surroundings. *Stop walking, and simply look.* Take the time to see, perhaps for the first time, the things which you may have walked right by, day after day. *Really **see** them, with no judgment.*

Allow your gaze to pause, as you "observe yourself looking." *Take your time.* **Breathe in the moment**. *It is all that there is. This one moment, followed by another, and another.*

When you are ready to move on, begin walking again, with grace and purpose. **Pay attention to your body as it moves**, *without any judgment or disapproval*. Only that it is moving, mindfully, your feet with each step firmly planted in the moment.

Observe each step, *independently and interdependently*. **Our actions can often appear to be independent, but they rarely are**. *Notice the interdependencies of your body* as it moves: *how one part integrates with, and often depends on another.*

Notice your body's rhythms… your breath in and out, your feet as they touch the ground, your arms as they swing back and forth. *There is an entire orchestra there which you are conducting.*

Be present with this observation for a while.

A good time to use this type of meditation may be when you are feeling too fatigued to sit, *or when you're ready for some fresh air for a change!*

JOURNALING ASSIGNMENT 9.1

Please take a few moments to describe your Walking Mindfulness Meditation

_____
_____
_____
_____
_____
_____
_____
_____
_____
_____
_____
_____
_____

METTA MEDITATION

Metta is another popular form of meditation that also stems from the Buddhist tradition. The word is often translated from its Pali (an ancient language used widely in Buddhist scriptures) origins as "loving kindness," and as a practice, **its goal is the cultivation of benevolence in the student, or practitioner**. *As a concept, metta can be found in ancient Hindu texts as well.*

In working with this practice of loving kindness, we repeat phrases that are representative of what we wish… what we want, for our own happiness and well-being… and that of others.

Metta meditation begins with oneself. *This is a must if we are to be able to offer genuine love to others.* After we have spent as much time as we need to with ourselves, our focus can shift to others:

- A benefactor, someone for whom we are grateful.
- A loved one, family or friend.
- Someone towards whom our feelings are neutral, perhaps a co-worker.
- Someone with whom we have experienced conflict and have not forgiven.
- All sentient beings, everywhere.

Traditionally, four phrases are used in a metta meditation. Here they are, and they, of course, can be modified in your practice to best represent your heart's desires in the most genuine way for you:

- May I be happy.
- May I be free of suffering and fear.
- May I be healed.
- May I be at peace.

It is possible as well when practicing metta to never leave yourself as the object of loving kindness. For instance, rather than focusing your attention on someone difficult in your life, bring that focus to a difficult aspect of yourself: one that you don't like or about which you continue to be judgmental. The objective, after all, is to accept, and forgive, with genuine love in your heart. It is not unusual that this won't happen at first. There are no failures here. Only opportunities to look deeper and love more.

ZAZEN

As Buddhism migrated to other cultures, its dogma changed accordingly, as did the practice of what we now call meditation. As it traveled to both China in the 6th century BCE, and to Japan in the 12th … the philosophy morphed into what we now call Zen Buddhism, and the meditative practice took the name of "zazen."

Zazen is a seated meditation practice, and its goal is *insight* into the nature of existence. *This is traditionally taught in one of three ways*: concentration, the study of koans, and just sitting.

Concentration is predominant in the initial stages of training... focusing, as in Vipassana, on the breath, *or on some other object of consistent attention*, building up the power of mindful concentration on just one thing, and is practiced in many Buddhist communities *(sanghas)*.

A sangha is a group of people who come together to study the teachings (dharma), and to meditate on them until there is some student experience of "samadhi," or *single-pointedness of mind*.

Once this state is attained, study progresses to **koan introspection**.

A **koan** is, characteristically, *a problem that is not solvable by intellectual reasoning*. **It is a riddle or puzzle used during meditation to help students unravel greater truths about the world, and about themselves.** *Its main objective is to shortcut logical thought, in favor of a direct realization of a reality **beyond** thought.*

They may seem like paradoxes at first glance. It is up to the student to tease out their meaning. Often, after a prolonged and exhausting intellectual struggle, the student realizes that the koan is *actually meant to be understood by the spirit and by intuition*, and not by logical reasoning. *Here's an example of a koan:*

JOURNALING ASSIGNMENT 9.2

The Sound of One Hand

"Two hands clap and there is a sound. What is the sound of one hand clapping?"
-Hakuin Ekaku

What do you think the sound of one hand clapping is?

_____

_____

_____

_____

_____

From here on, study focuses on awareness of the present moment. *Moment by moment, on purpose, non-judgmentally.*

The student does not use any specific object of meditation, but rather remains as much as possible in the present moment… aware of, and *observing what passes through their* Minds, and around them. **Thinking of not thinking**.

Non-thinking. *This is the art of zazen.*

TRANSCENDENTAL MEDITATION

Transcendental Meditation, with its roots in the Vedic traditions of India, was brought into the global mainstream in the 1950s by Indian guru Maharishi Mahesh Yogi.

It is a form of silent **mantra** *(most often a religious or spiritual thought/prayer)* meditation, practiced sitting comfortably, with eyes closed, and assuming no particular position from the yoga traditions.

The fundamental goal of TM is largely the same as with other meditation practices… to quiet the mind to a point where a greater clarity and focus can be achieved.

While training in TM requires a time commitment and financial investment, you may find some approximation of the clearing benefits of this practice by selecting a mantra that holds meaning for you *('Om Nama Shivaya' from the Hindu tradition is a good one, and means 'I honor the Divinity in all things')*… and, seated in a posture which is respectful to your body… say it silently, repeatedly, for 15 to 20 minutes.

You may want to journal about your experience, as well as with these other techniques. Mindfulness meditation continues to experience remarkable growth and popularity all over the planet, and today, as a spiritual practice it has also become increasingly legitimized within the *medical community* a development which has come in large part through the competent hands and creative mind of Jon Kabat-Zinn.

His leadership and passion have led the way in the development of a rigorous body of research focused on the physiological and psychological benefits of mindfulness meditation.

The results are staggering and have brought meditation into the mainstream of our healthcare systems.

Benefits have been found to include:

<u>Physical Benefits</u>

- Improved stress response, lessening of cortisol production rate
- Improved parasympathetic nervous system regulation
  (resulting in a relaxed state where the body can heal, repair and renew)
- Decreased blood pressure
- Decreased respiration
- Improved pain management

<u>Psychological & Emotional Benefits</u>

- Improved mood and sleep quality
- Improved concentration, attention, and self-awareness
- Reduced anxiety, depression, and impulsivity
  (improved neuro-chemical balance)
- Improved detachment skills
- Improved understanding of and control over thought processes

Meditation, in all of its many forms, is here to stay. We hope, if it's not already a daily practice for you, that you'll give it a try. As with any physical fitness training practice, there are certain elements of it that are foundational.

With regards to the spiritual dimension of your health, meditation will help you come to understand yourself better and provide a solid foundation for a more grounded life experience, allowing you to be more *consciously and holistically rooted in your mind, body, and Spirit.*

BREATHING
A full-mind, full-body force of nature.

Take a Breath

Breath is life! Breathing represents an important point of contact between mind and body, *since respiration occupies a unique interaction between the voluntary and involuntary nervous systems.* Shallow and irregular breathing reinforces stress and can have negative physical consequences. *Deep breathing, however, induces relaxation and promotes circulation.*

In our busy lives, we continually inhibit our natural breathing patterns in many ways, including habitual patterns of emotional stress. Conscious relaxation breathing relieves stress, allowing a return to natural, uninhibited breathing.

Background

For centuries, breathing exercises have been an integral part of mental, physical, and spiritual development in Asia and India. *Deep breathing continues to be an essential component of ancient Eastern practices, such as yoga and tai chi.*

Breathing techniques are part of a philosophical system that emphasizes balance and wholeness for achieving health. *Breathwork includes both stand-alone breathing techniques and those integral to other mind body practices.*

How Breathing Works

The primary purpose of breathing is to supply the body with oxygen and to remove excess carbon dioxide. The body's ability to produce energy and to complete the various metabolic processes depends upon sufficient and efficient use of oxygen.

Oxygen is necessary to help us repair and regenerate our bodies. *If any tissues in the body, including the heart and the brain, are deprived of oxygen for more than a few minutes, severe damage can occur.*

There are two basic ways of breathing: abdominal, *or diaphragmatic breathing, and* chest, *or thoracic breathing.*

Chest breathing *is relatively shallow.* The chest expands and the shoulders rise as the lungs take in air. Thoracic or *chest breathing is frequently a signal that the fight-or-flight response is activated even to the point of holding the breath or exhaling incompletely.*

People who have *chronic stress* tend to breathe either with their chest almost exclusively, or both with their abdomen and chest simultaneously.

Abdominal breathing *is deeper. Abdominal or* diaphragmatic *breathing involves inhalations that cause the diaphragm to contract and move down. Think of the diaphragm as an umbrella moving down then pushing upward into the lungs drawing air into the lungs:*

On your *inhalation*, air moves down into the lungs at the lower levels, the abdomen tends to distend slightly. This is the *inbreath.*

On your *exhalation*, the diaphragm relaxes and moves upward pushing the carbon dioxide out, and the abdomen moves back in. This is the *outbreath.*

Breathing abdominally helps bring air into the lower lobes of the lungs, resulting in an increase in beneficial oxygenation throughout the various cells and systems of the body. *We are born as abdominal breathers; it is our natural way of breathing.*

breathe **in**
calm.

breathe **out**
smile.

All things considered, what's most important with your breathing is your conscious awareness of it!

Benefits of Relaxation Breathing

The natural breathing process is a powerful coping technique for common anxiety and stress. *Slow, rhythmic breathing can turn an anxious mental state into one of relative tranquility and release the body from many other adverse effects of anxiety.*

Adjusting our breathing back to its naturally deep and slow way sends an instant message to the autonomic nervous system that there is no threat and the body can return to homeostasis *(normal balance).*

- When the body returns to a more balanced state, turning off the fight-or-flight response, a balance is created where the body can cure its maladies associated with stress.
- Deep abdominal breathing is not only effective in reducing levels of stress and coping with stressful situations, including test anxiety, but also in *reducing blood pressure.*

A number of studies have been done to show the effectiveness of deep breathing in turning off the stress response and, as a result, decreasing the symptoms associated with chronic stress.

Nearly every mindfulness meditation technique that is specifically created to reduce sympathetic nervous activity includes a breathing component.

CHAPTER 10

A Fully Conscious, Purposeful State of Mind

MINDFULNESS

Four characteristics, one state of mind.

One of the very best definitions of mindfulness, that focus of our awareness on the present moment, was written by a beloved teacher, Jon Kabat-Zinn, PhD. **Please memorize this short, specific and wise definition**. It will both test and help you every day as your conscious awareness continues to grow. *Mindfulness is:*

"Paying attention, on purpose, moment by moment, non-judgmentally."

Mindfulness is not a passive state of being. It is a fully conscious, purposeful state of mind in which you have chosen to engage in order to better yourself.

Let's pick this definition apart, for a moment, as it has a lot to say with a very few words:

Paying Attention. As Rick Hanson says in his beautiful book *Buddha's Brain: The Practical Neuroscience of Happiness, Love and Wisdom:* "attention shapes the brain." We are finding with increasing certainty that those things to which we pay concerted attention are the things which become hard-wired in our brains.

Paying attention asks us to observe and understand something or someone, in favor of trying to promote change.

On Purpose. On purpose is a state which is shaped by **intention**. There is then, nothing accidental about living a life which is defined in this way, as it requires focused thought first, in order to determine your intention(s) concerning one or perhaps multiple dimensions in which you choose to shape your reality:

- how you relate to yourself, to others and to the world around you
- how you choose your thoughts and actions.

Moment by Moment. Experiencing your reality in this way demands an increased awareness of your focus as time passes. Mindfulness is not a state that we can "freeze frame," but rather something more persistent; something that we choose to consistently maintain. It is not a goal. It is the journey, where, moment by moment we are dedicated to an awareness of our intentions, and consistently living them on purpose with every breath we take.

Non-judgmentally. It is easy to mistake judgment for attention, as we often consider that paying attention should be something of a critical state of mind. Mindful Attention is never critical. Judgment is, and it is often an unrelenting part of the chatter that goes on in our minds when we experience something, and immediately choose to categorize it. It arises from the **dualistic mind**.

The mindfulness of being non-judgmental is also an active, on purpose state, where we make a concerted effort to suspend the ego-based process of judging which runs on autopilot for many of us. Our need to judge is fed by the preconceptions which shape our personal world view: concepts, opinions, perhaps not even of our own thoughtful design—which, like a snake can strike, and poison with their venom.

In an instant your highest self can vanish into a dark landscape of name-calling, labeling, and condescension. The most effective defense you have from the pointless dis-ease of being judgmental is to **pause**… **pay attention** to what is happening, remember that you have chosen to live **on purpose**, and that in this moment we choose to live **non-judgmentally**.

This is mindful living. In many traditions, it is the lifelong quest whereby we find our best selves and live our best lives. **As you begin our study of mindfulness, ask yourself**:

"Why do I want to develop my ability to stay focused and aware throughout the day, and how can I train myself to become more mindful?"

Let's take a look at some highly-effective and time-tested mindfulness practices. As varied as the practices are, and the cultures, philosophies and wisdom paths from which they have originated, they are all in the service of your personal growth.

Behold this day.

IT IS **YOURS** TO MAKE.

– Black Elk

Bringing mindfulness into your life changes it in a number of holistic, spiritually healthy ways… and begins to embody a *living spirituality*. A living spirituality is a choice anyone can make, animating a higher goodness in your life with an *authentic reverence* for yourself, for all sentient beings, and for our Mother Earth. At first this may seem impossible to even comprehend, but with time, we believe that you'll notice how expansive you are becoming in your world view.

You'll begin to see this expressed as:

- Improvements in your ability to communicate with others, and to observe the world around you, fairly.
- Less confusion in your thought processes.
- Improvements in your ability to concentrate and focus on a particular task, conversation or hobby.
- Improved relationships with others.
- Improved confidence.
- Increased focus on loving kindness and consideration.
- Decreases in common outcomes of stress, e.g. elevated heart rate and blood pressure, mental confusion, irritability, and hyper-emotional behaviors.
- An increased ability to slow down the pace and increase the depth and breadth at which you experience your life.

MINDFULNESS FOUNDATIONS
Reflections on Jon Kabat-Zinn's 'Full Catasrophe Living'.

The life-changing practice of mindfulness gives us a new way of perceiving life in all its many dimensions. Mindfulness is a profound expression of human intelligence, one we experience on a beautifully gentle foundation of stability and possibility. Mindfulness practice is strengthened by the following principles. Before beginning a mindfulness meditation practice, we believe that you will be best served by drawing these concepts into your heart/mind as fully as you can.

Non-Judging
As in the nonjudgmental observation of your mind. It begins by taking a few steps back from yourself, *in order to become a more honest and kind observer of yourself.* As you do, watch carefully for the constant human tendency to judge internal and external events in your life.

Moment by moment, work to become acutely aware of any and all judgments that you are and have been making... *as you are making them*. Notice any labels you attach to events in and around your life. Begin to develop yourself as a person of a non-judgment, while becoming a *kind and curious observer* of life as it moves moment to moment. Notice how this practice leads to a more peaceful and relaxed body, mind, and spirit.

Patience

Patience is a form of wisdom. Everything in its own time, remembering that life unfolds only one moment at a time. Impatience never provides peace within, nor will it enable clear mental, emotional or spiritual progress. *Remember to remember* that each and every moment is a true moment in your life. Imagine a world where everyone was patient— how many changes would you see? How much smoother would life carry on?

Beginning with a Beginner's Mind

A beginner's mind is an essential mental framework for mindfulness. The challenge in keeping your practice pure is to keep your mind pure. **In Japan, they have boiled these two words down to one:** *shoshin*, **which means** *"beginner's mind."*

The goal of *shoshin* practice is, basically *to keep our beginner's mind in mind!* Imagine for a moment that you're coming home after a long, and tough day of school or work. To put it nicely, you're crabby. It would be easy to be unpleasant, but, knowing that they don't deserve that, you decide to enter into your shared space with a beginner's mind... calmly, and mindful that this moment isn't only about you.

How would that shift your experience (and everyone else's)?

In beginning to cultivate a sense of seeing and feeling into the richness in every moment, we are choosing to *look at each moment as if seeing it for the first time*. Our mind is open and *receptive to new possibilities*.

The beginner's mind is an attitude. When your mind is in a completely open state, you're *receptive and appreciative of new possibilities*, rather than basing your world view on personal opinions and judgments. Rather, each moment is seen as unique, with unlimited possibilities.

A beginner's mind is something that needs to be developed and nurtured. Start using this eye to the world in a variety of situations throughout your day. Choose to look at everything familiar with fresh eyes, and don't allow your preconceived notions or ego to enter your observation. Unclutter your mind. We believe that you'll begin to see things very differently.

Trust
This begins with you. Honor yourself, by trusting your intuition, your inner wisdom, your inner sense. Mindfulness will help you learn to connect with and trust in your own judgment, which begins to lead you toward a more trusting relationship with yourself, and others.

Non-Striving
Mindfulness meditation has no goal other than for you than to be yourself, paying attention to how you are in the moment—*however that is, by observing both your inner and outer landscapes simultaneously, in a fully relaxed way.*

Consider that perhaps the best way to achieve your goals is to back off from striving (not to be confused with becoming laid back). The goal is simply to begin to see and accept things as they are, *moment by moment.*

With *patience and regular practice,* movement towards your goals will take place by itself.

Acceptance
To cultivate acceptance, we need to be okay with looking at our life as it truly, honestly is at this moment.

Denial only forces a struggle within yourself. That requires energy, which in turn only begins to slow, and often completely disrupt our healing and growth. Fighting reality or holding on to old feelings or perceptions only creates a greater tension, and feelings of unease in your life. Once you accept things *"just as they are,"* then you can begin to move forward confidently. *Acceptance is an essential part of spiritual growth… a willingness to see things as they are, not as you wish them to be.*

Letting Go

Letting go is the cultivated ability to release the no longer important, no longer relevant thoughts, feelings, and situations that your mind wants to hold on to. Holding on to all of this only creates obstacles along the path to happiness. Letting go takes practice, beginning first with recognizing what you are holding onto, and why.

Once you identify your opportunities to let go, you can then begin to consciously release these mental constructs which are sabotaging you. This makes space... a spacious, uncluttered inner environment where the past, preconceptions, and judgments no longer have their hold on you.

An authentic personal world, where you have the freedom to see, feel, and act with clarity and acceptance.

MINDFUL WRITING
Writing with mindful intention, word by word, by word.

Mindful Writing is a wonderful way to open doors into yourself. *Into your truest self, by looking at any hidden parts of you that would benefit from seeing the light of day.*

Establishing our true intentions for actions upon which we decide to embark is an essential step in uncovering our highest good, because they motivate us. Bringing to light the underlying foundation for our life helps us to gain the clarity so often missing to us as we build our lives toward their highest possible potential.

Mindful writing is a technique and a skill available to you that can shed invaluable light upon your spiritual uncovering and development. In this experience, it will be helpful for you to consider your current relationship with writing.

Some people naturally love to put pen to paper, or fingers to keyboard... while others of us may feel intimidated or uncomfortable with writing anything at all. Such are the differences we share and hopefully honor as human beings.

No worries if you fall into the second group of reluctant writers. After you delve into this experience, we believe that you'll have begun to find exploratory writing to be a wonderful opening experience, so we hope you'll leave any discomfort aside and prepare yourself for a blossoming of your spirit and an opening of your soul in order to offer yourself a new-found freedom of, and love for self-inquiry!

As we begin to open the gates to our own mysteries, it's often good practice to open with a short invitation to Spirit for guidance, honesty, and humor…

> Dear highest good,
> may I be granted with
> the grace of guidance
> as I begin my practice of
> Sacred expression.
>
> From the depths of my soul,
> I can feel the support of eons
> holding me in safety and wisdom.

Something like that… after which, it is good practice to continue to expand your presence in the moment with a short mindfulness breath practice.

Sitting comfortably, but with a tall, relaxed posture that allows your breath to flow easily… take an easy in-breath, and say to yourself:

> Breathing in, I know I am breathing in.
> Breathing out, I know I am breathing out.

Do this several times to establish a regular, easy rhythm. With that, then repeat these words on your breath:

> In.
> Out.
>
> In.
> Out.

As you continue to do this, it may be helpful for you to place your entire awareness on either the rise and fall of your belly or chest, or if you prefer on the tip of your nose, as you observe and feel the bodily sensation of belly-breath movement, or air-body movement.

Continuing to place your full awareness on your breathing prepares you to stay present to this writing experience. Paying attention, on purpose, moment by moment, is what mindful writing is all about. If your mind wanders, return to your breathing, and placing pen to paper or fingers to keyboard, write down the first word or phrase that shows itself to you. As you continue writing, return yourself to this *clear space* periodically as you move along.

JOURNALING ASSIGNMENT 10.1

Put your entire focus on only one of the following at a time, until your thoughts feel complete, and on paper. In the process, stay as mindfully present with each word as you can. *They all count.*

Purpose. "I am writing to uncover my deepest spiritual yearning..." *(do you have questions about it? What are they?)*

_____

_____

_____

_____

_____

_____

Awareness. "As I write I am noticing..." *(of what are you most naturally aware, not aware?)*

_____

_____

_____

_____

_____

Acceptance. "As I write I am in full acceptance of…" *(what can you / can't you accept? Why?)*

_____

_____

_____

_____

_____

Gratitude. "As I write I am grateful for…" *(for what are you or could you be grateful?)*

_____

_____

_____

_____

_____

Appreciation. I am appreciating…" *(what do you or do you want to better appreciate?)*

_____

_____

_____

_____

_____

Affirming. "I affirm I am here to…" *(what is your sense of purpose in this life?)*

_____

_____

_____

_____

_____

As a next step, *choose someone to whom you would write a letter, and choose to express what you write from your highest good.*

It may be a letter asking someone for their forgiveness, or simply an invitation to join you for a special occasion, perhaps a hike, a movie or a meal. ***Before you begin writing***, *you might find it helpful to prepare by following the steps below:*

First, set a clear Intention for the letter. *What is it that you want to say?*

Second, discern deeply your motivation behind deciding to write this particular person. *What are your feelings about writing them? Can you write kindly?*

Third, create your writing space as a sacred place, infused with your highest self, *free of dissatisfaction, anger or shame. Accept your writing space and yourself, just as you are. Right now, in this moment.*

You're ready to begin!

As a last step, once you have completed your letter, mindfully pick up your paper, aware of your arm and your hand as you move to pick up the paper... slowly, carefully.

Remain mindfully present, as you read through your work one sentence at a time. Pause often, to fully take in the meaning of your message. If any corrections are needed, make them, without judgment, frustration or impatience.

Here are a few questions to ask yourself, and journal once you have completed this Mindful Writing experience.

 ## JOURNALING ASSIGNMENT 10.2

Take your time with your writing. *Be mindful of your choice of words.* As we've said, *each one counts.* So, if you want to tell someone that it was good to meet them, then by all means use the word 'good' as an honest descriptor for your meeting. Not everything is 'great,' nor is everything 'awesome.'

You'll find that the less you use more highly colored or emotionally charged words, the more meaning they have when you do use them.

Was this a difficult practice? *If so, why?*

_____

_____

_____

_____

_____

What else can you write about that will carry important value to you, spiritually?

_____

_____

_____

_____

One last thing. **Congratulations!**

MINDFUL EATING
Because eating is more of an experience than you may know…

Let's take an honest look, and some time to reflect on your style of eating.

We all need to do it. It serves a distinct purpose. We can be aware, fully aware of the experience, *or we can notice how often we are eating mindlessly and habitually.* It's outside of the scope of this book to discuss healthy eating, *but we **can** discuss eating mindfully.*

First of all, *a variety of clinical studies have shown pretty convincingly that mindful eating helps us feel better about our bodies:* preventing weight gain, coping with emotional (and other forms of "disordered" eating) and most importantly, to have an improved **relationship** with our food.

Spiritual practice is not just **sitting** and **meditation**.

It is looking, thinking, touching **eating** and **talking**.

- Thich Nhat Hahn

Most of us who live in a culture in which fast food plays a significant role rarely actually linger while eating... *to consider all the flavors, textures, and physical experiences that are going on as we eat.*

Too many of us inhale food, unconsciously.

Which presents us with a choice. Eating can be a mindful experience, or a mindless one. *In which group do you belong... mindless or mindful?* Before you answer, honestly, *let's be fair and take a quick look at the mindful approach, and let's take a look at your current approach (which may not be so mindful).*

JOURNALING ASSIGNMENT 10.3

To begin to better understand your personal approach to eating, take a few moments to reflect on it.

Begin with your morning. Take an inventory of your typical approach to breaking the sleep-filled fast of night before. Make a note if this pattern changes during the course of the day, and subsequent meals. *Consider and briefly journal:*

What do you do prior to eating?

_____
_____
_____
_____
_____

Do you plan in your head what you will be eating? Or make it up as you go?

_____
_____
_____
_____
_____

Do you attend to other things before eating? Or is eating first and foremost?

_____

_____

_____

_____

_____

Are you the kind of person who rushes through meals without giving the activity any attention?

_____

_____

_____

_____

_____

*Here's a few tips for **eating mindfully:***

- Set an intention to stay fully present and aware of each bite.
- Remember to bring in all of your senses… sight, smell, touch, sound and taste… into play during the experience of eating.
- Begin your mindful eating experience when you first touch either your utensil, or the food. In that moment, pause to absorb the 'look and feel' of either, or both (if you're having finger food).
- Take a moment to give gratitude for the food that you are so fortunate to have.
- Then, as you s-l-o-w-l-y bring the food up to your mouth, take a few moments to take in its aroma. How does it smell? They call food sustenance because it sustains you. It only seems fair that you can describe it with as much detail as you can. Just as effortlessly as you come to give thanks for it.
- Bring just enough food to your mouth to give you the chance to experience all of its flavors. Chew slowly, noticing (and we hope enjoying) all of the sensations of eating. What's going on in your mouth? Can you describe the texture of the food? Were you looking forward to it so much that you were salivating before that first bite? If it's spicy, does the spice follow your food after you've swallowed it? *These are the sensations of eating when you are present in the moment.*

Note: In his book *Full Catastrophe Living*, Jon Kabat-Zinn suggests first trying the above *with just a single raisin*. We think this is great idea for starters, as it limits the variety of textures and tastes that you're trying to mindfully process and describe. *We've found that working with other kinds of limited choices, like an apple for instance, works nicely too!*

The next time you eat, try keeping this in mind as a new focus on a new process:

Begin at the beginning. As you begin to prepare your meal, be present to preparing it. *Each step of it.*

Try to quiet your mind of other thoughts and distractions. If you're not preparing the meal yourself, ask if you can help, to become as involved and aware of the entire experience as possible.

Once your meal is in front of you, take a long pause, and bring into your awareness what each of your senses is telling you:

- **What does it look like?** What colors and textures catch your eye?
- **How does it smell?** Can you describe it? The seasonings that went into it?

Zero in on the part of the meal you want to taste first and pick up the utensil with which you will be eating it. Be present in this moment to the process of picking it up, gathering your first bite of food with it, and as it approaches your mouth smell it again before beginning to eat it.

Now go for it. Taste the first bite of your dinner. Take an inventory of what each of your senses is telling you about it as you begin to chew, now fully present with eating your meal.

- **How does it feel** as it touches your tongue? Is it rough, smooth, or something else?
- **How does it sound** as you bite into it? Does it sound at all?
- **Can you describe how it tastes?** It is simple, or complex?

Is this a different experience for you? What have you noticed about eating that you might not have given much consideration to before? Are you completely in this, and only this moment? Or has your mind already begun again to drift off into some arbitrary line of thought?

Once you're ready to swallow that first bite, is this party over? Not really. When you swallow your food, are you aware of it passing down your esophagus, and into your stomach?

Continuing to eat slowly and mindfully, are you aware of your stomach filling up with food, bite by bite? Or do you all of a sudden realize that you're full, and perhaps have eaten too much?

Each of these individual actions takes time to for your body and your brain to process.

This may be more of a challenge than it would appear at first blush, so you may want to begin this exploration with something less than a full-blown meal. Try this with just one food, perhaps something on which you'd normally snack. An apple, a grape, or a nut. Any of these would be excellent, less-involved choices.

At first, this exercise may seem pretty strange to you, but if you begin to incorporate mindful eating as a spiritual practice, you will be enhancing the often mindless act of eating in a very delicious way!

CHAPTER 11
Compassion

Compassion is the wish to see others free from **suffering.**

- the Dalai Lama

COMPASSIONATE LISTENING
Listening with intent, reverence, and integrity.

Compassionate Listening is a way that we can train our listening skills, in order to be fully present with what is happening in the moment, without trying to control it or judge it. As we let go of our inner chatter and habitual assumptions, we begin to listen—to honestly hear, with respect, and an intentional reverence to what is being said, moment by moment.

This is compassionate listening. *Listening with integrity.*

Does this take effort? Perhaps initially, but let's re-frame that, because, after all, *what's the point of giving someone your ear if it isn't fully in the hearing?*

It begins with having a contemplative mind: open, fresh, alert, attentive, calm, and receptive.

*Often, we don't have a clear concept of listening as an **active process**; but rather as something* passive and static. Truly listening with a contemplative mind means keeping it as open, vibrant, and *spacious* as it can be.

We're not trying to fix anything. We're only there to listen… sharing our time, open heart, and honest presence. Compassionate listening is an intentional skill, *cultivated through instruction and practice.*

It requires our full awareness. Paying attention to our rising thoughts and emotions, while maintaining focused attention on what we are hearing, *and abandoning our ego-based habit of listening with only the intent to respond, or even worse, to interrupt.*

It is **proactive** and *attentive, rather than **reactive listening**. A few powerful benefits of this listening skill are:*

- increased retention of the meaning behind the conversation
- improved insight
- clarity of understanding and meaning

JOURNALING ASSIGNMENT 11.1

The way in which we begin to engage in this kind of conversation is to ask clarifying questions, rather than offer our opinions, and the best way to do that is through practice. Let's begin by doing a little self-assessment of your current compassionate listening skills and attitudes.

What are three reasons why compassionate, mindful listening might improve your self-respect?

_____

_____

_____

_____

Identify four responses you have when you feel you are not being 'heard.' *Does this bother you? Why?*

_____

_____

_____

_____

In your own words, how you might change the way to listen to others going forward *(include your verbal, as well as your non-verbal messaging).*

_____

_____

_____

_____

From this moment on, I can see changing the way I listen by changing these things:

_____

_____

_____

_____

By doing so, I believe that these kinds of changes will occur:

_____

_____

_____

_____

SOUND MEDITATION
Expanding your listening skills.

Listening to sounds, whether those in nature, or man-made music, can have the same profound effects on our consciousness, as do the meditation techniques which we've previously presented, including:

- quieting the mind, and diminishing anxiety
- releasing trauma
- promoting presence and self-awareness
- relieving insomnia
- increasing our awareness of the deep connection between our inner and outer reality.

Let's try this out. Choose a place near you, if possible, outside and in a natural setting. If that's not possible, choose a place with which you are familiar:

Find a comfortable place to sit. Sit stable and still, like a mountain. Allow yourself to be relaxed, yet alert. Close your eyes, and simply listen intently to the sounds around you as they occur. No need to imagine, name, or analyze them. *Just listen to them.* The names you normally use to describe those sounds will arise in your head. *As they do, let them go.*

Listen now with an expansive awareness and notice how the sounds come to you.

- how do they touch your eardrums?
- how far do they travel within you?
- what does your heart have to say? what feelings, if any, wash over you?

If thoughts, emotions, memories or associations arise in your mind, notice them, *let them go*, and continue returning to the sounds.

Notice how they rise, then fall away. If there are no sounds, just listen and take in the silence.

Spend 15 to 30 minutes on this, and after this experience, ask yourself:

JOURNALING ASSIGNMENT 11.2

How do I normally listen in my daily life?

_____

_____

_____

_____

What are my listening habits?

_____

_____

_____

_____

Do I make judgments about certain sounds that I hear?

_____

_____

_____

_____

What helps me listen without judgment?

_____

_____

_____

_____

Now let's turn to music. There is quite a bit about each instrument that plays music, as well as the kind of music it is playing, that can affect your consciousness, and help to induce a clear, relaxed, and present state of mind. *Some of these musical factors include:*

- incorporating simple harmonies and unadorned melodies
- using repetition to help induce a state of trance
- using dynamics to help heighten mood
- using silence to open up space, and provide room for reflection
- keeping rhythms to a minimum.

Listen to a recording of each of the following five sacred music types, and describe what feelings arise in you: *joy? anxiety? fun? happiness? sadness? thrill? laughter? Something else entirely? You are sure to find examples of each in a YouTube search:*

Gong Bath_____

Reed Flute (Native American) _____

Pan Drums _____

Gregorian Chant _____

Beethoven's 3rd Symphony _____

The gift of hearing is a blessing, and listening, *really listening,* can be a profound, life-changing experience, and worth a mention in our gratitude journals.

SELF-COMPASSION
The challenge of overcoming self-criticism.

Over the past twenty years, many students and clients have admitted how difficult it is for them to overcome the constant self-criticism that led to unsettling negativity in their lives.

It's probably fair to say that we've all been there, but one of the wisest ways to stop this inner dialogue is by giving ourselves the Divine gift of human kindness. It's brilliant in its simplicity, really—but in the moment, all too easy to forget.

So, here's an easy-to-remember acronym to help you *remember to remember* that compassion begins at home…

Take a few moments a day, every day for the next week, and walk yourself through the **BRING** *acronym.* See if it begins to help you self-reflect a little bit more kindly:

Be mindfully present as you wrap yourself up in a warm blanket of pure kindness and compassion for yourself, *as if you were calming yourself as you would a newborn child.*

Reflect tenderly and mindfully on what is happening in your mind. No judgment, no self-flagellation, just pure, gentle awareness. The mind can be a subtle trickster. *Pay close attention to your:*

Inner landscape and notice the *state of your emotions* and your *physical response* to these emotions.

Now bring full concentration to the sensation of your breath flowing in and out of your nose, instead of listening to the inner voice, *and experience your breath as expansively as you can.*

Grin or smile as you exhale… *and feel the comfort wash over you.*

Feel free to share **BRING** *with friends and family,* because as far as loving ourselves goes, we could all use a little help from time to time.

COMPASSION FOR OTHERS
When honesty with ourselves leads to compassion for others.

Journal this exercise about at least three, preferably four people. Recite each step silently to yourself, but directed toward the other.

For the purpose of this exercise, one should be a stranger, another must be a family member with whom you have "issues," and one must be an individual who has done you wrong, and who is still present in your memories. *Then write about each of your experiences.*

Here is your step-by-step list of recitals. The sequence is the same for each person you have chosen:

Step 1 With attention on the person, repeat to yourself:
"Just like me, this person is seeking some happiness for his/her life."

Step 2 With attention on the person, repeat to yourself:
"Just like me, this person is trying to avoid suffering in his/her life."

Step 3 With attention on the person, repeat to yourself:
"Just like me, this person has known sadness, loneliness, and despair."

Step 4 With attention on the person, repeat to yourself:
"Just like me, this person is seeking to fulfill his/her needs."

Step 5 With attention on the person, repeat to yourself:
"Just like me, this person is learning about life."

JOURNALING ASSIGNMENT 11.3

Now, on to your journaling. Tell us about your experience with each.

About the stranger

_____

_____

_____

_____

_____

_____

_____

_____

About the family member

_____

_____

_____

_____

_____

_____

_____

About the one who hurt you

_____

_____

_____

_____

_____

_____

_____

_____

-adapted from: Harry Palmer
Resurfacing: Techniques for Exploring Consciousness

INTEGRATING OUR SHADOW SELF
Making friends with our greatest life-long teacher.

In looking at the parts of us that live in the shadows, the beloved psychologist Dr. Carl Jung brought to light one of the most critical elements of the human experience... _that our perception of ourselves is often not as fully integrated on a conscious level as we would want to believe._

What is the shadow, actually?

According to Jung, our shadow consists of energy patterns, known as *selves* or *sub-personalities* that were *disowned* — *pushed down into our unconscious in childhood, as part of our coping strategies.*

Our shadow is actually often a *collective*… parts of ourselves that we have chosen to either hide or deny. Sub-personalities that we have rejected or disowned, and which we have buried in our subconscious mind, often very early on in our life, *as a way to better cope with who we want to be.*

So, if that works for us, why even look at it, and consider working with it? *The benefits can be many,* perhaps the most important of which is a deepening of our genuine, most authentic self *through learning to re-integrate these hidden aspects of ourselves into the greater whole…* and in the process, learning to be loving and kind to those parts of us that we have buried, regardless of the reasons why. *It is, then, a practice in self-compassion and self-love.*

Working with our shadow self can eventually allow us to become more compassionate… first and foremost, to ourselves, which allows us, in turn, to be more compassionate with others. *This can be a significant challenge.* We need, in the process, to look at dimensions of ourselves which are at our very core: our world view, our self-worth, and our values.

It is a process that asks no less of us than to invite these strangers back into our lives, embrace them as weaknesses, and turn them into strengths. We begin by re-introducing them to the light, understanding that it is **us** that have held them in the dark as unlovable or unworthy.

Doing this allows us to stop projecting those aspects of ourselves, those that we have chosen not to embrace and own… onto others… and instead begin to accept our "perfect imperfection" as our own.

This is not easy work. It asks that we look, honestly—at our deepest, darkest secrets. That we look at them in the mirror and ask ourselves what triggers our behaviors. *When we become angry, why? When we dislike someone, why? When we judge, why?* Is this a part of ourselves that we don't like, and *are we actually just judging ourselves?*

Is it worth considering that what we perceive as our personal reality is really a reflection of our inner life? *Taking all of this into deep discernment can yield the richest of insights.* This is shadow work, and it can be incredibly rewarding.

And yet, many people run away from their shadow work. It is far easier to live in the safety of our *imagination and illusion* than to meet, head-on—those less-than-ideal parts of ourselves, rather than putting all of our cards on the table, so that we can begin working towards developing our highest selves.

Whether we like it or not, though, our shadow is our greatest teacher. If we can **mature** enough to befriend our fully-integrated selves... the "good, the bad and the ugly" of us, then we can begin to move into our deepest personal honesty. This brings often life-changing insights that allow us to develop our self-awareness, and the authenticity of our world view.

Note: while this practice can often be self-administered, it's important to understand and acknowledge that if you come to experience in this process any chronic, or seriously troubling feelings about yourself, it is always best to consult with a licensed medical practitioner who is trained in helping you with this work.

JOURNALING ASSIGNMENT 11.4

Let's take a moment now to test our spiritual courage, on the path towards a more evolved life.

Bring to mind someone in your life who really "bothers" you, or who has characteristics which you find unlikable, destructive or distasteful. Ask yourself what exactly it is about them that you don't like. *What are the specific qualities in them that bother you so much?* **Once you identify what bothers you, ask yourself:**

> "Am I uncomfortable with this person, or am I really recognizing
> something I dislike in my own past or present?"

Stay with that insight for a while. *This is where we begin to mine the gold of shadow work.*

Next, personalities aside, are there any specific situations in which you find yourself where you consistently feel this strong energy of dislike or discomfort? **Ask yourself the same basic question:**

"What am I uncomfortable with here?"

Gather your thoughts, journal your answers, and for each, ask yourself as honestly, openly and courageously as you can:

"Have I ever exhibited that same quality because of my own actions? The quality that I so strongly dislike in another?"

If the answer is yes, *you are on to an important area of personal transformation!*

Keep going. *When did, or when does your reaction to this unfavorable quality materialize in you? What were the circumstances?* **Take some time now to write about this, as well as the previous questions you've asked yourself. If this is an honest assessment, it's likely that by the time you're done, you'll have re-introduced yourself to a part of your shadow.**

Our shadow is our great teacher. Holding compassion for yourself as a human being who remains "perfectly imperfect," you can now begin to move into your honesty, while developing your skills in support of a more non-judgmental self-awareness.

Beginning to have a more consistent relationship with your shadow side, by increasing your awareness of it eases its control over your perceptions of self-worth, relationships with others in your life, and your world view.

_____

_____

_____

_____

_____

_____

_____

_____

_____

_____

_____

_____

_____

_____

_____

_____

_____

_____

_____

_____

_____

_____

CULTIVATING SPIRITUALITY IN RELATIONSHIPS
More than meets the eye …

We've discussed at some length that, in many ways, spirituality is setting an intention to give our full attention to our inner selves. Looking in, finding ourselves, and who we really are. Determining our unique, authentic understanding of the world—our world view. Not the view we've inherited from birth, but ours.

If you haven't spent time yet doing this reality check, it is well worth it. Why do you look at the world the way you do? From your own unique life experience, or because you have inherited those views from your family, friends, or your past and present relationships?

Because once we look outward with that genuine, authentic understanding, filled with personal integrity, our spirituality has a real chance to blossom. *We begin to see and/or feel ourselves in a higher, sacred light*, as French philosopher and Jesuit priest Pierre Teilhard de Chardin so brilliantly proposed:

> *"We are not human beings having a spiritual experience,*
> *but spiritual beings having a human experience."*

It is with that understanding that we begin to better understand our connectedness.

Plant the love of the holy ones **within your spirit.**

Don't give your **heart** to anything but the **love** of those **whose hearts are glad.**

\- Jalaledin Rumi

We see that each of us has unique connections with ourselves. That there is both light and dark within, and that they both exist in something of an eternal dance. Lovers, in a way. One cannot exist without the other, and so each needs to be known as a dimension of who we are… not cast aside as something that we aren't because we believe that others would not approve.

When we have made this honest, spiritual connection with ourselves, we have paved the way to have higher understandings of, and hopefully—reverence for our relationships with others. Relationships that have more potential for our personal fulfillment than we could have ever otherwise imagined.

A question we always find helpful when meeting someone new, is this: "How can I enrich this person's life? How might they enrich mine?"

In either case, the answer may very well lead nowhere… *that there is no potential there.* It is often worth a second meeting, to see if feelings and initial observations prevail. If so, it may be time to move on. If, on the other hand, things seem promising, you've likely made a highly informed decision, based first on our own self-acceptance.

No matter what the nature of the relationship is: romantic, platonic or professional… it now has the opportunity to be based on several very rich and satisfying premises:

It serves a higher purpose. It acknowledges that spirit is creative at its core, that it is constantly evolving, and that as a result… *so will the relationship.*

We are willing to take ego out of the equation. The value of the relationship is not rooted in to what degree each partner's personal needs are met. *Rather, the goal is always to work together towards the greatest mutual good*—and eliminating the concepts of winning and losing in our relationship helps assure that outcome.

Honesty, and honest communication, prevails. We choose to see ourselves as we really are. We choose to see the world as it really is. We seek the truth that exists outside of our personal lenses of perception. Colored only by itself, and not with the paints of our own, often subjective palettes.

There is a personal dedication to authenticity. We may, each of us, fail from time to time. And that's okay. We just need to acknowledge that as something approaching an eventuality, and that when, not if, it happens—we need to *own* it, and communicate *through* it. Failing is nothing more than the opportunity to try again, *and it will happen when the relationship is dedicated to creative growth.*

Through all of this, it can be easy to lose track of ourselves. *It can also be easy at times to project who we are on the other.* So it's important to bear witness to ourselves, as a basic mindset. A few thoughts to consider as key elements of our own ongoing reality check:

Who owns the responsibility for your happiness? Remember that we are continuously re-wiring ourselves, and in the process we are also re-wiring our relationships. How we react in any given situation begins that process.

The degree to which your reaction persists becomes the degree to which your brain is changing—how you view your partner in the relationship, and how they view you. The greater the degree to which this happens can dramatically increase your likelihood to blame, while radically decreasing your ability to look in the mirror.

Are you willing to receive? Are you willing to give? This is a huge growth area in pursuing the fertile ground of spiritual relationships.

We normally do one better than the other. In accepting that as a premise, choose to accept that as well as normal. *Self-judgment is not constructive,* nor is it necessary.

In receiving, we take an inherent risk, if we are living with an open heart. We may feel unworthy, and reluctant to be gifted. We may be hurt by an unkind word. Unintended, but more than possible in the heat of the moment.

In giving, our partner takes inherent risks of the same nature.

In both, though, if we honor the relationship on its highest, most solid foundation, we accept both acts as sacred. We are willing to hold love, kindness, generosity, disappointment, anger… all in equal measure. *We live in trust.* Distrust, on the other hand, is an energy killer, *and no one has time for that!*

This kind of sharing lives from one to the other as **a leap of faith,** where we each trust that the other will gently hold what they give or expose about themselves without judging or shaming them—*and we do so in sacred trust.*

It is also a sacred gift, to be fully present to another as they open their heart mind and soul, *and invite us into their world.*

This is the very special connection that spirituality brings to our relationships. Where we are able to begin to see our interconnectedness, and the reality of impermanence. Where we can more easily see the importance of the highest truth and integrity in our relationships, as we begin to more mindfully present to them.

JOURNALING ASSIGNMENT 11.5

Please share your thoughts on this topic of Spirituality in Relationships. *How does the concept relate to the relationships, past and present, successful and failed, in your life?*

_____

_____

_____

_____

_____

_____

_____

_____

_____

_____

_____

_____

_____

_____

_____

MAY YOU MOVE
to the next life
with ease.

- Marion Woodman

LEARNING HOW TO FACE GRIEF

The phases of grief in times of great loss.

We all process grief in our own ways. Some are helpful and lead to healing, while others can be seriously unhealthy and best avoided. We grieve using the best tools we have at the time, in the moment.

As good as many of these tools are, our ability to use them in the moment is colored significantly by our relationship with the one for whom we are grieving.

We often haven't had to get through much of our life before we lose another to whom we are emotionally attached. Years later, in looking back, one of the ways in which we see a relationship with clarity is through our memories of *how we have grieved* for the loss of another, and *which ones come to the surface first.*

Here is one of Constance's:

> "I was a junior in college when my father died unexpectedly. He was at the height of his career... a visiting scholar at Northwestern University in Evanston, Illinois. I was a music major, and at the time, fortunate enough to be spending the Fall quarter in Germany, Austria, and Switzerland looking for a music conservatory where I could complete my degree in vocal performance.
>
> *I learned of his death by telegraph.*
>
> I don't think that I've ever felt so alone, confused, and angry. My whole world was upside down, and I was completely inconsolable.
>
> Gathering my things, I booked the first flight home, expecting only to get there eventually, and to cry in the meanwhile. As it turned out, I was on my flight next to a lovely gentleman who could see that I was having a rough time.

While I was content to sit and play solitaire all the way home, he gently asked if I played gin. I responded yes, and he said, 'Well then, we'll play cards all the way to Montreal.' And then, before he dealt our first hand, he asked me, 'Would like to talk about the pain you are feeling?'

I burst into tears, telling him that my father had just died, and that I really didn't know what to do. And he then took my hand and said, 'May I share a tragic story of my own?'

'I lost my wife and our two daughters in an automobile accident last year.'

Until we landed in Montreal, my loss was in perspective, and I understood that I was not alone in my grief, or my loss. That was his final destination. For me, only a connection.

On the last leg of my trip, alone now, I had no idea how my life was not going to crumble into a million unrepairable pieces. My father was my rock. Seemingly, a lot of the confidence that others saw in me was a projection of the assurances that he had always given me.

Where was the courage I needed to do this by myself now? My insecurity was as overwhelming as my pain. I started drinking. *And I drank a lot.* My grief was drowned, a day at a time. I began to believe that the pain was going away, *until I realized that I wasn't really dealing with my grief at all, just tucking it away.*"

This story is not unique. The relationship was, of course. But the concept of loss is universal, and we are often unprepared for it. We know that alcohol and drugs are of no value to us in these situations, and yet it is an easy way out, and makes the pain seem less in the moment.

Grief rituals exist the world over… but oddly, in the American culture, we are often left to our own devices. Fortunately, the 70s brought us vital research on grief… and we now have a much better roadmap from which to maneuver through this life-changing, difficult process.

One such guide, and one of the seminal books on this subject of death and grief was written by Dr. Elisabeth Kübler-Ross, a Swiss-American psychiatrist, who in her book, *On Death and Dying,* lays out her theory of the five stages of grief:

1st step: Denial

We are in denial when the reality of a situation is at odds with what we prefer it to be.

We are overwhelmed. There must have been a mistake. Life begins to make no sense. We go numb. We ask ourselves: 'why go on… and how can we?' We try to find a way to simply get through each day. This helps us cope, actually, and allows us to take in our feelings of grief in much smaller, more manageable doses.

There is a spiritual grace in this. And as we begin to accept the reality of our loss, as we ask these questions… we begin to heal. The more we do, however, the more the feelings that we have buried come to the surface. And so, we enter the next step.

2nd Step: Anger

There is nothing left to deny. It is real, this loss. We become angry, frustrated, and want to somehow assess blame. It is important that we feel this anger. The more we express it, the more it begins to dissipate.

Our anger knows no bounds, and even extends to that which is greater than us… our God, if you will. *Where has this God been, to have let this happen?*

The anger is healthy. Underneath it is our pain. The pain which we have tried to bury.

3rd Step: Bargaining

This isn't particularly rational, but this third stage involves the hope that we can somehow avoid the cause of our grief. Maybe a better lifestyle. We are drowning in 'what-if' and 'if-only' questions. We want to strike a bargain so that things can be different, and the pain goes away. We want life back the way it was.

Of course, these kinds of questions only serve to point us to some fault with ourselves. It keeps us locked in the past, where unfortunately, done is done.

4th Step: Depression

Once we try, and ultimately fail at bargaining, our attention can move into the present. We feel empty. Our grief is fully exposed and expressed. We are depressed and feel as though it may never end.

Again, this is actually healthy. We are now dealing with the magnitude of our loss in an honest, healthy way. We withdraw. That is natural as well. To be otherwise is not.

Depression at this time isn't something about which to feel guilty, to be fixed, or to be snapped out of. It's just healing.

5th Step: Acceptance

This is not the same as 'being okay.' We don't usually feel okay about loss. We will never like this reality now as much as the one which is now gone, but we can learn to accept it, and live with it. It is our new normal, and the past is now filled with moments where memory serves. No longer intact as it was, but accessible in a new way. We learn to carry on in new ways. *Learn new things, take responsibility for others.*

Maybe finding acceptance is just having more good days than bad ones.

But we begin to live again. At first, perhaps feeling like we are betraying the one we've lost. We haven't. We can never replace them, but we can live. Make new connections, develop new relationships, and once again invest in our relationship with ourselves… and grow into something we may not have been before.

And we realize that there we have reached this moment only when we have given grief its time. *All the time it needs.*

We all die. And as much as it is important that we understand the grieving process when dealing with our own grief, it is equally important when others are in need of our support.

So here are some things that are appropriate and not appropriate to say in support of someone who is grieving:

Appropriate things to say to someone who is grieving:

> I am so sorry for your loss.
> I wish I had the right words, just know I care.
> I don't know how you feel, but I am here to help in any way I can.
> You and your loved one will be in my thoughts and prayers.
> My favorite memory of your loved one is…
> I want you to know, I'm here for you and always just a phone call away.
> Say nothing. Give a hug instead.
> We all need help at times like this, I am here for you.

Not so appropriate things to say to someone who is grieving:

> At least she lived a long life. Many people die young.
> He is in a better place.
> She brought this on herself.
> There is a reason for everything.
> Aren't you over him yet, he has been dead for a while now?
> You can still have another child.
> She was such a good person, God wanted her to be with him.
> I know how you feel.

We've always loved these words from the Bhagavad Gita:

> *"The Spirit is beyond destruction.*
> *No one can bring to an end the Spirit, which is everlasting."*

Spirit knows no loss. And so, grieving, while difficult and painful, is only a path to healing, not an eternal obligation to suffering. *And perhaps, as spiritual beings, we will all, lost loved ones included, have a human experience once again.*

ON DEATH
Kahlil Gibran

You should know the secret of death.

But how shall you find it unless you seek it in the heart of life?

The owl whose night-bound eyes are blind unto the day cannot
unveil the mystery of light.

If you would indeed behold the spirit of death, open your heart wide
unto the body of life.

For life and death are one, even as the river and the sea are one.

In the depth of your hopes and desires lies your silent knowledge of the beyond;

And like seeds dreaming beneath the snow your heart dreams of spring.

Trust the dreams, for in them is hidden the gate to eternity.

Your fear of death is but the trembling of the shepherd when he stands
before the king whose hand is to be laid upon him in honor.

Is the shepherd not joyful beneath his trembling, that he shall wear
the mark of the king?

Yet is he not more mindful of his trembling?

For what is it to die but to stand naked in the wind and to melt into the sun?

And what is it to cease breathing, but to free the breath from its restless tides,
that it may rise and expand and seek God unencumbered?

Only when you drink from the river of silence shall you indeed sing.

And when you have reached the mountain top, then you shall begin to climb.

And the earth shall claim your limbs, then shall you truly dance.

CHAPTER 12
Some of Our Favorite Spiritual Practices

Kindness in WORDS creates **confidence.**

Kindness in thinking creates **PROFOUNDNESS.**

Kindness in **giving** creates LOVE.

- the Dalai Lama

RANDOM ACTS OF KINDNESS
What happens when we step away from our needs.

"Practice Random Acts of Kindness." Although some may dismiss it as just saccharine new age, bumper sticker wisdom… it's much more than that. *It's a reminder to be just a little more kind, and a little more gentle, and that best begins with ourselves.*

There is real science behind kindness, *rooted deep in our physiology.* There is a high in performing acts of kindness, whether as an act directly expressed to another a **person,** through our volunteerism at a **place,** or even another **sentient being**—*our cats, our dogs, even our house plants.*

JOURNALING ASSIGNMENT 12.1

Acts of kindness flood our bodies with feel-good hormones such as serotonin and endorphins, which, in turn, sets us up to want to do it some more, *because it feels so good.* In its own way, *performing random acts of kindness is a very highly spiritual practice.*

So why not take this opportunity to see for yourself? **Perform three random acts of kindness. Describe them, and the responses to them in detail:**

with a Family Member

_____

_____

_____

_____

_____

_____

_____

with a second Family Member or alternatively, a Friend

_____

_____

_____

_____

_____

_____

_____

with a Stranger

_____

_____

_____

_____

_____

_____

_____

Describe any feelings that arose within you in offering, and in response to offering an unexpected kindness. Did it matter whether or not the other person showed their appreciation? Would you consider continuing this as a practice? If not, why not?

_____

_____

_____

_____

_____

_____

_____

KINDNESSES IN WAITING
Sort of like an embarrassment of riches, only different.

JOURNALING ASSIGNMENT 12.2

List a dozen acts of kindness that could benefit anyone: friends, family, even strangers:

1 _____
2 _____
3 _____
4 _____
5 _____
6 _____
7 _____
8 _____
9 _____
10 _____
11 _____
12 _____

LECTIO DIVINA
A delightfully insightful spiritual practice.

The History

Lectio Divina, which is Latin for 'Divine reading,' is a traditionally Catholic practice, the original purpose of which was to increase the knowledge of God's word through scriptural reading, meditation, and prayer. Its roots can be traced back as far as the 3rd century BC.

The Practice

The practice of Lectio Divina consists of four separate steps: *read, meditate, pray, and contemplate.* We've found the steps much easier to remember thanks to the way in which father Thomas Keating (one of the architects of the practice of centering prayer) has recast them for our time: *read, reflect, respond, and rest.*

Lectio *("read")*

The practice begins with the slow and gradual reading of a scriptural passage, perhaps several times, so that the words are thoroughly internalized. Passages are often read with this degree of repetition, where each reading brings focus to a different segment within the passage, allowing the reader to consider several possible meanings.

Meditatio *("meditate")*

After completing the readings of the passage, it is time to then take it into our own discernment, not with the goal of analyzing it, but rather of waiting for the meaning to come to us through a direct communion with Spirit.

Oratio *("pray")*

Remembering that in the Christian tradition, prayer is a dialogue with God, this step underlines our understanding of the scripture we've read, that we know it is *of God*, and that we embrace it *with God*.

Contemplatio *("contemplate")*

This is the time for our silent (contemplative) prayer, where we express our love of God, and that we have heard His word with our full attention.

While Lectio Divina has its historical focus on gaining communion with Scriptural passages, it can be applied to our spiritual practice as well. *Let's take a look at how that is done:*

Here's a step-by-step process to get you started with this wonderful practice:

Preparation

Choose a passage from any spiritual text you would like to deepen into today. We're including some here as guidelines, and as a point of departure for you in this practice.

Prepare **a sacred space**... a special environment filled perhaps with things like inspirational photos, or gentle, preferably instrumental music.

Give yourself some centering, calming time (1-5 minutes), following each of your breaths... breath, by breath, by breath... with mindful awareness to calm yourself intentionally.

Read

On your first reading, read the entire passage out loud, slowly. Pay attention to any words, phrases or concepts that capture your attention. Write them down.

Reflect

Go back to your notes and meditate on everything that's caught your attention.

Read the text again, this time to yourself. Meditate on these questions:

- *For **what** am I truly grateful?*
- *Do the same words or phrases jump out at you?*
- *If so, what is it about them that is speaking to you in the moment?*
- *What is it saying to you about your life today, if anything?*
- *Do the words or passages define something of who you are today, or something that is missing within you?*

Respond

Now, begin to ask questions of Spirit, bringing it into conversation.

If the same words have jumped out at you again and again, it is no coincidence. So, tell Spirit what has come to mind as you meditated on them. Share your thoughts on the matter and tell Spirit about your hopes as a result of your readings. Will your better understanding now serve to open your heart with yourself, and with others?

Rest

Finish your practice by acknowledging that you have a need and an opportunity for change.

In this process, that which has resonated most with you has been gifted to you, in the presence of all that is. You have embraced your connection to something greater than yourself, to which you have an inextricable connection. You have pointed out your best path for change, have acknowledged your understanding, and have given thanks.

Lectio Divina is a wonderful practice.

Read, Reflect, Respond, and Rest

Here are some sample passages for you to reflect on using Lectio Divina. Most of them here are short, with the notable exception of the Desiderata by Max Ehrmann, which we believe you'll find to be a real bonanza for use in this practice! Its name comes from the Latin, meaning 'desired things.'

"The secret of health for both mind and body
is not to mourn for the past,
worry about the future,
or anticipate troubles,
but to live in the present moment wisely and earnestly."

-Buddha

"A new commandment I give you: Love one another.
As I have loved you, so you must love one another.
By this all men will know that you are my disciples,
if you love one another."

-Jesus of Nazareth
John 13:34

"The best and safest thing is to keep a balance in your life,
acknowledge the great powers around us and in us.
If you can do that, and live that way,
you are really a wise man."

-Euripides

Knowing others is wisdom;
Knowing the self is enlightenment;
Mastering others requires force;
Mastering the self needs strength"

-Lao Tzu

"Character cannot be developed in ease and quiet.
Only through experiences of trial and suffering
can the soul be strengthened,
vision cleared,
ambition inspired
and success achieved."

-Helen Keller

Desiderata

Go placidly amid the noise and haste,
and remember what peace there may be in silence.
As far as possible without surrender
be on good terms with all persons.
Speak your truth quietly and clearly;
and listen to others,
even the dull and the ignorant;
they too have their story.
Avoid loud and aggressive persons,
they are vexations to the spirit.
If you compare yourself with others,
you may become vain and bitter;
for always there will be greater and lesser persons than yourself.

Enjoy your achievements as well as your plans.

Keep interested in your own career, however humble;

it is a real possession in the changing fortunes of time.

Exercise caution in your business affairs;

for the world is full of trickery.

But let this not blind you to what virtue there is;

many persons strive for high ideals;

and everywhere life is full of heroism.

Be yourself.

Especially, do not feign affection.

Neither be cynical about love;

for in the face of all aridity and disenchantment

it is as perennial as the grass.

Take kindly the counsel of the years,

gracefully surrendering the things of youth.

Nurture strength of spirit to shield you in sudden misfortune.

But do not distress yourself with dark imaginings.

Many fears are born of fatigue and loneliness.

Beyond a wholesome discipline,

be gentle with yourself.

You are a child of the universe,

no less than the trees and the stars;

you have a right to be here.

And whether or not it is clear to you,

no doubt the universe is unfolding as it should.

Therefore, be at peace with God,

whatever you conceive Him to be,

and whatever your labors and aspirations,

in the noisy confusion of life keep peace with your soul.

With all its sham, drudgery, and broken dreams,

it is still a beautiful world.

Be cheerful.

Strive to be happy.

-Max Ehrmann

PRACTICING LECTIO DIVINA

Tell us about your practice.

JOURNALING ASSIGNMENT 12.3

After having practiced Lectio Divina using the examples above, please tell us about three of the keywords or phrases that particularly resonated with you, and what they suggested to you, and how they suggested to you a path for change.

SEEING SPIRIT
Encountering the Divine through imagery.

Visio Divina ("Divine seeing") is a corollary practice to Lectio Divina, a method where we pray (have a dialogue with spirit) based on our observation of art, images or other visual media.

Visio Divina has a more established heritage in eastern Christian orthodoxy, but it's important to note that the Word of God has often been expressed through imagery, and perhaps even more importantly—we now live in a media-rich world. We express ourselves in sound bytes and 15-second media clips. So perhaps Visio Divina is an emerging practice in western culture, one that is rooted in imagery, but one which asks us to slow down and really observe in an involved way.

It is easy to see the similarities between this practice, and Lectio Divina. We are asked to see with beginner's eyes and beginner's minds, laying aside our preconceptions and judgments, and listen to God's word as it speaks through the imagery.

Visio Divina can be a personal practice, or one which is shared with others. You don't need to go anywhere to do this, although a change of scenery is often welcome if available. The steps here are really the same as with Lectio Divina:

The first step is to prepare. Settle into a comfortable posture, breathe into clarity, eyes closed, and ask spirit to join you in these moments of contemplative prayer.

Visio (see)

Look at the image, icon, graphic, drawing or photograph that you've chosen. Take it all in but notice what parts of it catch your eye most. After you've spent some time with it, close your eyes.

Meditatio (meditate)

Now open your eyes and re-visit the imagery. Let your eyes be drawn where they are drawn naturally. Close your eyes again and try to see just that one part of the image to which you are so drawn. Spend some time with this in your mind's eye.

Oratio (pray)

When you're ready, open your eyes and again find that part of the image to which you are so attracted. Find a way to associate it with a feeling, or a word, or even another image. When you've found it, close your eyes once again.

Ask yourself, in this silent moment of communion, *what is spirit trying to say to me? What am I supposed to learn from this?*

Contemplatio (contemplation)

Open your eyes after a few moments, and take in the entire image, and how it relates to the portion of it that has caught your eye.

Ask yourself, *what emotions does this image evoke in me? Why?*

THE SPIRITUAL PRACTICE OF HAIKU
Authentic thought, genuine heart.

A traditional Japanese haiku is a three-line poem composed using a total of only seventeen syllables. The first line contains *five syllables*, the second line has *seven syllables*, and the last, *five syllables* again. Haiku often focuses on images from nature, and is a wonderful, often spiritual exercise in simplicity, intensity, and directness of expression.

It doesn't need to rhyme *but can if that is the way you choose to express yourself.*

A little history. Haiku, as simple as the form is evolved from something quite different and very involved, called *renga*. Renga was a collaborative poetry practice where an entire group of poets would contribute a stanza, and a director would guide subsequent contributions, suggesting specific words or topics to be incorporated… sort of like a 13th century version of Mad Libs™!

A *haiku* was originally the opening stanza of a *renga*. It broke off as its own form 300 years later, and traditional haiku is still remembered today for the work of its early masters, including Basho, Buson, Issa, and Shiki.

Contemporary or modern haiku, sometimes referred to as American haiku, has opened up this highly-choreographed art form into something just as expressive but different. *Here's two examples:*

Silently,
Gazing skyward,
God appears.

-C. McClain

Heavens awakened,
Gazing, as
Sand-lit fire sleeps.

-C. McClain

Can you feel the spiritual essence within them? What triggers a spiritual feeling for you?

Although it is good practice to *first, cling to the traditional structure* of writing a haiku (learn the rules, before you break them), the 5-7-5 syllable structure has been largely dismissed by American haiku writers. This isn't because we believe that we have a better idea, but rather because the fundamental building block of Japanese haiku, the *mora*, really has no equivalency to our English *syllable*.

Haiku was originally always written in the present tense, and it would often pit highly contrasting images against one another. What survives today is a focus on a simple, often unlikely moment in time, a scene, painted with often highly-contrasted images, and which plays out in the briefest of moments.

Both are beautiful means of spiritual practice and artistic expression.

Again, for comparison:

Modern Haiku

Losing its name,
a river
enters the sea

-John Sandbach

Traditional Haiku

Without a within,
dimension has no meaning
once Spirit is lost.

-James Anthony Walker

Both immediately paint a scene… simply, directly, and intensely expressed. Traditional haiku adds the extra dimension of working with the rules it imposes, and for some, that is a welcome personal challenge, but in either case, haiku is more than the practice of minimalism in writing.

It is good spiritual medicine, and an excellent spiritual practice for seekers at almost every age.

JOURNALING ASSIGNMENT 12.4

Please share with us three of your most spiritually uplifting Haikus … one in traditional form, and two in contemporary form:

_____

_____

_____

_____

_____

_____

_____

_____

_____

MUDRA
Triggering our state of consciousness.

Have you ever been in a yoga class, and seen the instructor or other people put their hands in weird positions and wondered what they mean, or more importantly, whether you should do the same? **Why are Mudras important in yoga?**

Mudras are specific positions for our hands, fingers and/or bodies that we can use to trigger moving our awareness in a desired direction. *Mudras offer us a significant spiritual and energetic connection to a specific, desired state of consciousness.* **Mudra is a Sanskrit term meaning "seal."**

Each finger represents an essential element, chakra, anatomy, emotion, and quality in mudras:

- **Index finger:** Air, self-worth, heart chakra, mental, lungs, large intestine, depression, sadness, grief, the Individual Soul
- **Middle finger:** Space/heaven, responsibility, throat chakra, heart, circulatory and respiratory systems, impatience/hastiness, ego
- **Ring finger:** Earth, relationships, root chakra, liver, gall bladder, nervous system, anger, illusion
- **Little finger:** Water, communication, second chakra, kidneys, fear, karma
- **Thumb:** Fire, self-assertion, stomach, worry, the Supreme Soul.

Fun Fact: *Did you know that there are over 100 Mudras (108 to be exact)?*

108 is a special number, which has held, and continues to hold both mystical and geometrical significance all over the world. *If you're intrigued,* you may want to research it on your own, as it's more than we can go into here …

And so, back to mudras.

Most of us are familiar with "prayer hands," the position of our hands when we pray. **This same hand and finger placement is known as the Namaste Mudra** in yoga communities. Let's take a few moments, and try it in practice:

Draw your hands evenly together, matching left and right as closely as possible. Then position them directly in the center of your chest, or what is known in many Eastern traditions as the **heart center**, and in the East Indian yogic tradition as the heart, or **Anahata** (4th) chakra.

We are crossing cultures here, which may not be familiar territory for you, but please try to stay as open-minded throughout this practice as possible.

Once you've positioned your hands in the Namaste Mudra, *take three gentle breaths and try to observe yourself from the outside looking in.* In other words, *try to visualize your physical body as if you were someone else standing next to you, looking at you. What does your kind and nonjudgmental observer see? What shape or form is your physical body taking?*

Spend some time with this. *Become conscious of your breath.* Be aware of your in-breath, your out-breath, *and the space in between the two.*

Notice also what you are manifesting physically, and how you are feeling emotionally. *Did your posture change when you connected your hands in this way? Did your head bow toward your hands in a show of deep humility and respect? Did anything else shift within you?*

Has your mindset, your world view, shifted in any way? *Do you have a different sense of yourself and your holistic Presence than you did before exploring this mudra?*

Beliefs about the spiritual power of mudras originated from the various Buddhist, Hindu and Yogic traditions of the last millennia. Today, they remain a powerful tool for *integrating your mind, body, and spirit,* and for increasing your *receptivity* to a more awakened spirituality.

Let's take a look at a few of them.

For this practice we ask you to stay in each mudra for at least two minutes or more. As with the Namaste mudra, allow yourself to breathe gently, carefully observing any energetic effect each mudra may have, as consciously and non-judgmentally as you possibly can.

Some mudras are easy to create, while others may require more practice because we are not accustomed, in our day-to-day life, to assuming certain positions for our fingers and hands. No worries, you'll succeed shortly!

Mudras can be explored while sitting, standing or lying down.

As we said, mudras are designed to increase our spiritual and energetic connections to a specific, desired state of consciousness, directing that energy in very highly defined, concerted ways. **Try these, and make note of your reactions:**

COMPASSION and CONCENTRATION (Jnana or Gyan Mudra)

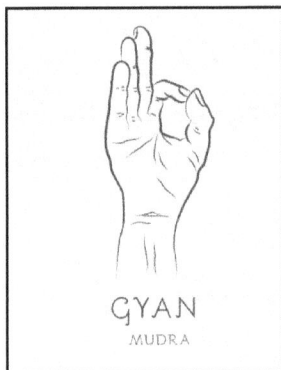

GYAN
MUDRA

This familiar mudra, the Jnana Mudra (the wisdom seal) is practiced to raise our consciousness and to deepen our compassion for ourselves, and others. *All* others.

Connect your index finger and thumb softly but securely. *This will create a teardrop-like shape.* The remaining fingers are drawn together, pointing upward. Notice that your hand is cupped, as if ready to receive an offering.

DIVINE WORSHIP (Anjali or Namaste Mudra)

The Namaste mudra helps to alleviate anxiety and stress, helps concentration, and is often used in meditation because it helps maintain the meditative state. *(see more detail above)*

The palms are pressed and sealed tightly together with the fingertips pointing upwards.

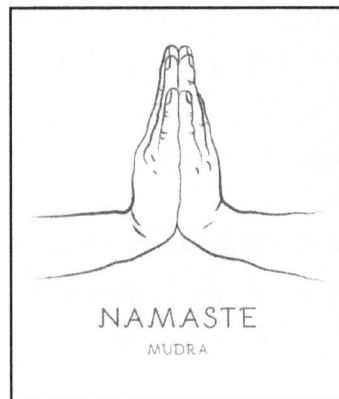

NAMASTE
MUDRA

CALM (Pala Mudra)

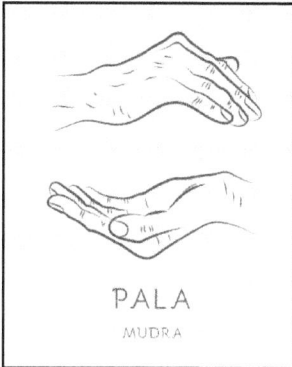

PALA
MUDRA

This mudra brings an awareness of your Solar Plexus, a place of trust and personal power. If you're feeling anxious, this practice can help you calm and center yourself.

The palms of your hands are slightly cupped, and face each other, one above the next.

PEACE (Abhaya Mudra)

This mudra demonstrates a sense of fearlessness, protection, peace, and friendship.

The right hand is held open and faces out at shoulder height with a twisted elbow.

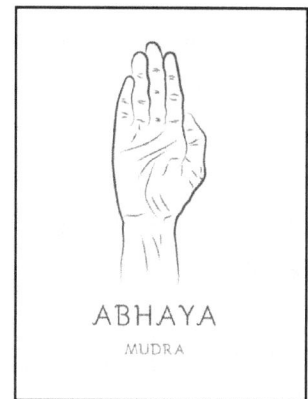

ABHAYA
MUDRA

LIFE FORCE (Prana Mudra)

PRANA
MUDRA

The Prana mudra is the mudra of life force, giving us more energy.

Bend the ring and little fingers to touch the tip of the thumb, while keeping the other two fingers stretched out.

Mudras are triggers. Incorporating them into your spiritual health practice is useful in reinforcing your desired outcomes and can be incorporated into any of your mindful activities, whether that might be your yoga routine, your meditation practice, or any other of your regular exercises in mindfulness.

MANTRA
The spiritual power of sound.

A mantra is a short spiritual phrase to call upon the highest power of which we can conceive— whether we call that power the Ground of Being, the Ultimate Reality, the Self Within, or God.

*Mantras are similar to **Affirmations**.* Affirmations, are short "I Am" statements meant to affirm something that we want ourselves to be, that we're not. For example: "I am fit."

Even if we're a couch potato, we are affirming the change we want to see in ourselves... even before we've done the work to achieve our goal. *Both mantra and affirmation are amazingly powerful tools to use to bring about change.*

Whatever name we use, in repeating the mantra, we call forth what is best and deepest in ourselves. While rooted in religious dogma that is alive and well across the planet, mantra is a powerful contemporary *spiritual* practice as well.

The word mantra comes from the Sanskrit language, and when we break it down, we see that the root is "man-," which means "to think," and that the suffix is "-tra," which means tool or instrument. *So literally, a mantra is a "tool of thought!"*

Mantras are useful in *energizing our intentions*. They are like seeds, only mantras are planted in the fertile soil of practice. As with so many spiritual practices, when we nurture them consistently over time, they will bear the fruit of your intention.

The benefits of practice don't end there. By steadying the mind and reminding yourself of a deeper view to your world, repeating your mantra with consistency can help you come back to a place of inner peace, well-being, and calm.

Those feelings have their roots in real physiological change, and include:
- lowered blood pressure
- restored digestive system balance
- relaxation of the nervous system
- relief of muscle tension

- relief of insomnia
- reduction of the pesky monkey mind
- release of fears
- lessened symptoms of depression
- increased optimism, self-esteem, and confidence

Mantras can be physically, emotionally, and spiritually transformative, and those changes come as a direct result of our enabling *(and thereby increasing)* **the neuroplasticity of our brains** *(we'll discuss this mind-blowing concept of neuroplasticity in a later chapter).*

Mantras have served the world for thousands of years and can be found in all of the world's religions, East and West. **Let's take a look at some of the most widely used mantras in the world today.** *If one from your current, former or desired wisdom path works for you, that's always a good place to start:*

Mantra:	Baruch Atta Adonai
Religion:	Judaism
Origin:	Hebrew
Translation:	I honor the Source who blesses me

Mantra:	Om Mane Padme Hum
Religion:	Buddhism
Origin:	Sanskrit
Translation:	I celebrate the Jewel at the Heart of the Lotus

Mantra:	Om Nama Shivaya
Religion:	Hinduism
Origin:	Sanskrit
Translation:	I honor the divinity within all things

Mantra:	La Ilaha Il'Allah
Religion:	Islam
Origin:	Arabic
Translation:	Other than God, there is nothing

Mantra:	Kyrie Eleison
Religion:	Christianity
Origin:	Greek
Translation:	I call on your compassion and mercy

Mantra:	Wakan Tanka Toka He Ya
Religion:	Lakota Sioux
Origin:	Sioux
Translation:	I pray to great Spirit first

What we would want to believe is the very simplest of mantras is actually one of the most deeply expressive: **Om** *(which you will sometimes see spelled Aum).* **Om is said to be a 'seed' syllable from which the entire cosmos arose.**

Om is both a sacred sound and a spiritual icon in many Eastern Indian wisdom paths, and often used as a mantra in and of itself in Hinduism, Buddhism, Jainism, and Sikhism. Its icongraphy is fascinating, and its meaning incredibly deep:

A - the awakening of life.
U - the living of life.
M - the ending of life.

In other words, **all that there is, ever was, or ever will be.** And so, when we initiate our meditations by using the Om mantra, we connect with the absolute, the ineffable.

Do mantras need to be rooted in religion?

Absolutely not. Mantras do not need to be theistic. **They should however meet two basic guidelines:** that they have a spiritual component to them, and that they resonate with you as the practitioner.

Can I make up my own mantra?

Of course! We would suggest that, when designing your own... you consider these four guidelines for success:

- express it in the positive/affirmative
- express it in the present
- express it simply - *less is more!*
- let the energy of the positive promise you are creating resonate with you completely and convincingly.

JOURNALING ASSIGNMENT 12.5

Please share with us a mantra of your own design:

_____

_____

_____

_____

Again, *personalized affirmations* **are useful when you want to set an intention in the moment**: "I am strong," for instance, is a powerful affirmation to engage both before and during any kind of physical activity, *particularly one where you feel challenged, and uncertain of success.* Repetition will help establish and maintain a connection to the state you wish to cultivate during your activity.

It's been said that in yoga, **asanas** are the postures of the body, and that **mantras** are the postures of the mind and so are more like positive affirmations, which *can help keep you connected to a particular state of mind.*

Mantras are powerful, *just like you.*

MANDALA MEDITATION
Creating the universe as your sacred space.

The word "mandala" has its origins in the classical Indian language of Sanskrit. While it can be loosely translated as "circle," *it is far, far more than that.*

In many spiritual traditions, **mandalas are a useful tool to establish a sacred space for ourselves,** *and also as a means to achieve a mindful, meditative state.*

Mandala patterns have been used as an integral part of highly diverse religious traditions all over the world for centuries: from Buddhist monks, to Christian nuns, to the natives of the Americas.

One thing they share in common is that they are all are objects which exist to invite mindful states for reflection and discernment. The Navajo (whose non-anglicized name is *Diné*), and Tibetan monks alike, half a world apart, create sand mandalas to demonstrate the impermanence of life. Taoists contemplate the yin/yang within the circle as a study in the differences, as well as the interdependencies of life.

And so, mandalas, even in their most simple form, can be a representation of the universe itself: simple, yet highly complex in how interdependent their designs are. How we choose to view life is captured in each and every one: whether we choose to see our world from a macro or a micro perspective, we discover how deeply interconnected that world really is when we immerse ourselves in these intricate designs.

That truth has been lost on few, once they have studied mandala as a tool for spiritual and personal growth:

> "[A mandala is] a safe refuge of inner reconciliation and wholeness. [It is]
> a synthesis of distinctive elements in a unified scheme representing the basic
> nature of existence."
>
> -Carl Jung

Mandala Meditation provides us with a rich and mindful opportunity to step away from all of our distractions and enter into the depths of a relaxing silence.

In approaching this practice, you can either purchase a book of mandalas, which are easy to find online or in brick and mortar bookstores, or you can create your own. You'll also find mandala software available online, which allows you to author your very own mandala designs, easily, but the easiest way to begin is to pick up pre-made patterns to color *(and some booklets are as cheap as $1.00)*.

We recommend colored pencils for your mandala practice, so once you've found some of those, selected your mandala pattern (or the one here), and have found a quiet place to create your sacred space, *you're ready to begin.*

We've given you one here with which to start your journey. *Enjoy!*

CHAKRA OPENING FOR HEALING
A Divine spiritual tool for increasing self-awareness.

Many of us in the west have either heard of, or tried experimenting with the Hindu chakra system to help begin an inner awareness exploration in the pursuit of our well-being and health.

Chakras help us connect our bodies to our spirituality. Think of each of the seven chakras as energy fields that are aligned in an ascending line from your tailbone, all the way through to the top "crown" of your head.

They are energy points with your body that you can "see" using your imagination, imagery, and an open felt (somatic) sense that will develop as you develop your practice. Once you begin to notice your energy body, you'll notice that it is slightly bigger than your physical body... in other words, it surrounds you.

All the chakras are associated with actual, specific, functions and our habitual thought patterns, emotions and behaviors.

Chakras are often described as spinning wheels, or discs of energetic points located within the human body to assist the movement of our energy, known in India as "*Prana,*" and also 'Chi' in other Asian countries.' From a western standpoint we call this same energy *'vital energy' or 'life force.' It's up to you to decide which word or phrase works best for you.*

The *chakra system* recognizes when human energy flow becomes blocked, and through practice, we can consciously interact with them to help us find our healthiest state of physical, emotional, and spiritual balance.

Each chakra represents an aspect of higher consciousness that is essential to a person's life, and each has a physical, emotional, creative, and celestial component... so at a basic level, *a person's emotional and physical health is directly dependent on well-functioning chakras.*

When a distortion occurs in one's chakra balance, it usually arises from stagnant energy in a specific energy center and can sooner or later negatively impact us physically or psychologically.

When we make a correction to our chakra balancing, a corresponding change will show up elsewhere in our body. When we block an experience because it was unpleasant or emotional, we also block the corresponding *positive emotion* that we gain by a well-functioning chakra. It may get clogged with stagnant energy and spin irregularly or in the wrong direction.

We want to be high-functioning human beings, and the chakra alignment process is a beautiful way to connect our spiritual awareness to one of our body's innermost and esoteric communication systems.

When our chakras become distorted, it usually means that we are creating a reality that we believe to be valid, but which is in actuality something that we have manufactured, often based on previous life experiences.

We want to keep all seven of our chakras open and receptive to our life experience in the moment, in order to remain fluid and balanced, no matter what upset might have knocked us off into the waters of uncertainty.

Here's a chart showing the seven chakras and their approximate position in the body. Each one has a corresponding energetic color related to it. If you'll notice, the progression from the root chakra to the crown chakra also corresponds to the energetic colors in the visible spectrum of light.

Here's a brief description of each:

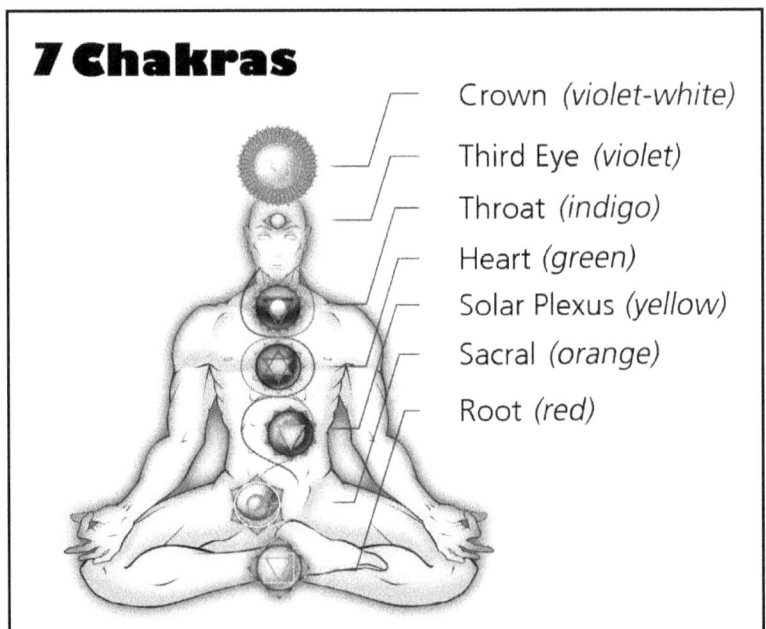

7 Chakras

Crown *(violet-white)*

Third Eye *(violet)*

Throat *(indigo)*

Heart *(green)*

Solar Plexus *(yellow)*

Sacral *(orange)*

Root *(red)*

The 1ˢᵗ or Root Chakra

The Root Chakra is located right at the bottom tip of your spine and is your foundational chakra.

When opened fully you'll feel grounded, but if it's blocked you might experience serious life issues, such as overwhelming feelings of instability. Its balance is critical in keeping us safe and secure, and it also helps us align to our physical health.

The color for this chakra is red, and is symbolic of energy, courage, confidence and change.

The 2ⁿᵈ or Sacral Chakra

The Sacral Chakra is located in your lower abdomen, two fingertips beneath your navel.

When opened, this chakra serves to help us connect with others in a fully accepting way. It also keeps us open to new experiences and allows our passions and pleasures to manifest. If blocked, you may be struggling with finding pleasure and following your most passionate pursuits.

The color for this chakra is orange, which is symbolic of creativity and sexuality.

The 3ʳᵈ or Solar-Plexus Chakra

The Solar-Plexus Chakra is located in the area right under your ribcage and breast bone, or sternum.

This chakra relates solidly to your self-confidence. If blocked, you may be feeling blocked in your life in general, exhibiting feelings of low self-esteem, self-worth, or self-image.

The color associated with this chakra is yellow. It symbolizes clarity and confidence.

The 4ᵗʰ or Heart Chakra

The Heart Chakra is located in alignment with your lower and upper chakras, and of course, with your physical heart.

This chakra opens to love, while releasing any negative beliefs onto which you may be holding. In balance, it will help you let go of harmful relationships or patterns, releasing negative energy. If blocked, you may struggle to find inner peace, happiness, and joy, and you may close yourself off from opening up to new relationship opportunities.

Green is the color associated with this chakra. It symbolizes emotional stability, and our ability to express love, compassion and forgiveness.

The 5ᵗʰ or Throat Chakra

This chakra is located above the heart chakra, in the proximity of your throat.

It represents your ability to clearly and effectively communicate your thoughts and feelings. If this chakra is open and clear, you'll feel confident in expressing yourself in many areas of life, able to remove old patterns and fears, allow for more loving communications, and the establishment of respectful social boundaries.

If blocked, you may find self-expression a difficult direction to take, and you may have issues with both telling the truth and accepting the truth from another.

The color of this chakra is indigo, and it is symbolic of our ability to communicate with ourselves, and with others.

The remaining two chakras are considered our higher-order spiritual connectors. If you have a regular meditation or prayer practice, these centers will be familiar to you. If not, you may find those practices useful in accessing these chakras.

The 6ᵗʰ or Third Eye Chakra

This chakra is located right above the bridge of your nose.

Hold your middle and index fingers together, place them on your lower forehead, *and you'll have found your third eye!* When this chakra is open, you can see the bigger picture of life all around you, losing untrue impressions of yourself and becoming more realistic with your life. If it's closed, your imagination, insight and intuition will suffer. You may have trouble making decisions, and your head might feel thick, cloudy, and dull.

Violet is the color of this chakra, and it symbolizes intuition and wisdom.

The 7th or Crown Chakra

The Crown Chakra is located at the very top of your head.

It is the highest energetic point in your body, allowing you to open to spiritual guidance, God, a higher Source, or a universal energy. In this way, you are open to Divine guidance, and to seeing the world as a whole… a world of equality, kindness, and care. If this chakra is blocked, you will feel detached from your spirituality, faith, and the world as a planet born to peace.

Violet/White is the color of this chakra, and it is symbolic of creativity, self-awareness, and spiritual connection in unity with all sentient beings.

A Chakra Awareness and Opening Practice

Let's take a look now at we can know if we have a blocked chakra.

We start with familiarizing ourselves with our energetic body. Give this simple awareness technique a try:

Set an intention to feel and/or see all your chakras. See them in an open and receptive presence within you and surrounding you energetically.

Visualize each chakra as the energetic, spinning disc that it is. See all seven as open and *vibrant* in full color, beginning with your root chakra (grounding you initially) and then moving upward sequentially through all the energy centers. Once you've reached your crown chakra, reverse the process, moving back down one chakra at a time, to your root.

Your goal here is to get to the point where you can 'move your attention' from energy center to energy center, with ease and fluidity. If you notice 'sticking' points along the way in this practice, *those are an indication of blocked energy.*

Make notes so that you have a good idea where you need to spend your time in alleviating these blockages.

Now let's work on opening them up! This is the process of chakra balancing, and while it can be an involved process, there are some simple and fun ways to start. Remember that each chakra is different, and each deals with different life issues:

It's important at the start to s*et an **intention** to feel/see all of your chakras in an **open and receptive presence within you, including the energetic space surrounding you.** Then begin to focus on each that you perceive as being blocked:*

1ˢᵗ Chakra - *you need to ground yourself.* One of the best ways to do that is to literally enhance your connection with Mother Earth. Get barefoot and take a walk. Find a tree and connect. You get the idea.

2ⁿᵈ Chakra - *you need to connect with your passions.* Sometimes, our ability to do this is blocked by feelings of inadequacy or shame. So perhaps a cleanse is in order. Try a long bath, or a shower. Get into the ocean, or a pool. Relax, enjoy yourself and let go.

3ʳᵈ Chakra - *try some exercise.* Anything, really. Just move. If you can get outside to do it, all the better.

4ᵗʰ Chakra - *find a way, an easy way, to open up your heart.* If you have a love for books, read one by a favorite author. If you have a pet, spend time with it. Their love is unconditional. In short, spend time doing what you love. Feel no guilt. Just do it.

5ᵗʰ Chakra - *write something. This blockage is about opening up your authentic lines of communication.* Write about your day. Write about a day that would be your perfect day. Make it big, and bright, and compelling, and convincing.

6ᵗʰ Chakra - *find a way to see the big picture.* We've discussed the physiological and psychological benefits of it, and its ability to stop the chatter in our heads. It works. Spend some time with it. When the chatter goes away, that's the time when we have clarity to see our big picture, and that's what this chakra is all about.

7ᵗʰ Chakra - *build on your meditation with affirmative prayer.* Prayer is, of course, often something associated with religious wisdom paths. That doesn't need to be the case, and it can offer us a way to open up this highest of chakras.

Think of it as an affirmation of your greatest good. A statement, not a question. An accomplishment, not a request. Think of it as your own, unique part in making life, as you wish it to be… manifest. We do this by connecting with Spirit directly… in conversation, *agreeing between the two of you that what you seek is already a divinely done deal.*

JOURNALING ASSIGNMENT 12.6

Try this scanning for blockages practice, and once you've identified a blockage, try one of the exercises we've suggested. *Write about the experience:*

_____

_____

_____

_____

_____

_____

_____

_____

_____

_____

_____

_____

_____

_____

_____

_____

BEGINNING EACH DAY WITH GRATITUDE
In its absence, we miss much that life has to offer.

Gratitude is a quality we can feel when we are *thankful to another* for something they have done on our behalf.

Gratitude is also an *attitude we can choose to embody.* For example, we can make a spiritual decision to begin each day with a short gratitude practice. To make this practice natural for you, we suggest either making or buying yourself a lined journal where you can make daily entries.

In practice, establish and persevere with this simple routine.

Once you are fully awake, take three to five minutes to sit down in a quiet place. Close your eyes gently, relax your breathing, and ask yourself two questions:

- *for **what** am I truly grateful?*
- *to **whom** am I deeply grateful for being in my life (past, and present)?*

Although we encourage you to make your routine repetitive, *your journaling should **not** be.* This should be a living record of that which has transpired **daily** for which you are grateful.

Gratitude is a powerful element in establishing forgiveness—gratitude helps us to 'pay it forward.'

This "attitude of gratitude" is an amazingly transformative practice. When we take the time to really recognize all we are deeply grateful for in our lives, we can quickly begin to see how fortunate we are, and this allows us to deflect and even eliminate all of the unnecessary and hurtful narratives in our heads that often hijack our highest self.

When we think of that highest or higher self, we begin to see ourselves as better human beings in what is far too often a nasty, spiteful world. ***Living an intentional, spiritually engaged life feels lighter.*** And life is easier because of the personal growth that comes through practices like gratitude.

Science supports this, thanks to the efforts in recent years that in large have been spearheaded by **The Greater Good Science Center** *at the University of California, Berkeley.* Their research work, with focus on key interdimensional areas of human health, personal, and relational well-being have shown that individuals who engage in a regular, consistent gratitude practice:

- have stronger immune systems and are less prone to depression
- experience more joy, optimism, and happiness
- develop stronger relationships, and exhibit more generous behavior
- exhibit less frequent feelings of loneliness and isolation.

Self-assess your GQ (gratitude quotient) by taking their online quiz. It will help you determine if you're truly grateful for the good things in your life—or you tend to take them for granted. *There's no pass or fail here… just a way to provide you with a benchmark as you continue your walk down the spiritual path.*

Your quiz results will be scored online and presented to you. Based on your score, you will also receive a list of recommended activities that would benefit your gratitude practice, based on their research findings. And your results (completely anonymous) will also help advance their studies even further for which they will be extremely grateful!

The link is: https://greatergood.berkeley.edu/quizzes/takequiz/gratitude

JOURNALING ASSIGNMENT 12.7

Tell us a little bit about how you did, which one of the exercises you tried, which they recommended for you, and your feelings about the practice:

My score was: _____ **out of 105**

The exercise I tried was: _____

My feelings about the exercise are:

_____

_____

_____

_____

_____

_____

_____

_____

_____

_____

_____

_____

_____

_____

_____

_____

_____

_____

_____

_____

_____

_____

_____

_____

_____

_____

_____

_____

If we really want to learn **how to love,** we must learn how to **FORGIVE.**

- Mother Teresa

THE HEALING POWER OF FORGIVENESS
Casting aside the emotional weight we carry.

> *"The bitterest tears shed over graves are for words left unsaid and deeds left undone."*
>
> -Harriet Beecher Stowe

There are few quotes that we know of which encapsulate the pain at the end of a life than the one we've quoted above, because it is so very true. It is a time, after the last time where we have the chance to make peace with one another. To say what needs to be said. To release the weight that we carry in our relationships before it magnifies into unmanageable, irreversible regret. Often that may only take three words:

> *"Please forgive me."*

In the study of the healing power of forgiveness, it is almost unnecessary to go beyond the teachings of the Buddha. The psychology of Buddhist practices on the topic of forgiveness are deeply rooted in one simple, honest premise: that, as human beings, we suffer. And that with courage, we can suffer less through learning to forgive... forgiving others, or being forgiven ourselves. Forgiveness is not for the faint of heart. It demands our sincere emotional courage, and our emotional strength.

Each of us would indeed be unique, if not totally blessed, to go through our lives without having been caused pain. Without having been hurt, betrayed, belittled or cast aside. Unique as well if we haven't done any of the same to another. No matter the root cause, no matter the degree big or small, we suffer as a result. That was no surprise to the Buddha. The Second Noble Truth tells us that it is we who are the cause of our suffering.

Forgiveness is the only way to release this pain, and as importantly release us from a past, which prevents us from fully moving on with our lives.

Forgiveness from a Buddhist perspective is not a moral imperative. To the contrary, it is if nothing else... practical. It is a way to lighten our emotional load, and in the process, improve our spiritual and mental health.

Forgiveness, again from a Buddhist perspective, is a practice. Practices achieve their *mastery* and best effect with repetition. *So how do we begin a practice of forgiveness?*

Beginning with a personal commitment to honesty, we are best served by starting from within, with ourselves. Once a month, once a week, once a day, practice forgiving yourself. If you are being honest with yourself, you probably have some material to work with!

For some, even practicing forgiveness on ourselves can be difficult. But with practice, you will soon begin to notice a change within. A lighter feeling about yourself. Maybe even a lighter outlook on life.

From there, things get a little bit more complicated, but if not *perfect*... practice *does* make a difference. Since we are being practical here, you might choose to begin by making a list of the people in your life who have hurt you, and what they did that caused you pain and hurt.

As you take just one of them into your forgiveness practice, meditate on *why* what they did hurt. As you relive this moment, take note of how you are feeling, holistically. That is to say, in the whole of your mind and body. Is your emotional heart closed from pain? Is your body clenched from anger? These things are your baseline in this practice with this person.

This is the point where the Buddha said:

> "If someone has abused you, beat you, robbed you,
> abandon your thoughts of anger.
> Soon you will die.
> Life is too short to live with hatred."

It is at this point where we need to begin to look at the other, not ourselves.

When this happened, what was going on with them? What was happening in their life? Was it under their complete control? Or were they suffering, and because they were... they hurt you?

Because, as much as we like to believe that we understand another, we never really know how their life story is playing out for them in any given moment. And if that rings true for you as a concept, then there is a real possibility that they *deserve your compassion, not your anger.*

Life, as a manifestation of the infinitely creative universe in which we live, is a series of adjustments. A forgiveness practice is a key component in whether these adjustments are infrequent, major, and potentially debilitating, or minor, "scheduled maintenance."

JOURNALING ASSIGNMENT 12.8

Take this opportunity to journal some specifics. First about you, and then about just one other person that you might try to forgive:

YOU

For what behavior have you had a hard time forgiving yourself?

_____

_____

_____

Where do you carry the memory of this in your mind/body?

_____

_____

_____

If this behavior is directed towards someone else, have you made amends?

_____

_____

_____

Have you reflected on your behavior and learned from it?

_____

_____

_____

Are you the same person as before?

_____

_____

_____

Is it time to show compassion for yourself?

_____

_____

_____

ANOTHER

Person to forgive (first name only):

_____

Their behavior:

_____

_____

_____

Why did you feel hurt/violated?

_____

_____

_____

Where in your mind/body do you feel the emotional experience of what they did?

_____

_____

_____

How long have you felt this way?

_____

_____

_____

Is it time to forgive and let go? _____ **If yes, forgive and let go.**

How do you feel?

_____

_____

_____

_____

_____

CHAPTER 13

The Sum Total of Our Existence

How people treat you is
THEIR KARMA.

How you react is **yours**.

- Wayne Dyer

ADDRESSING KARMA

The sum total of your existence.

From the Beloved Irish poet John O'Donahue:

> *"If you send out goodness from yourself, or if you share that which is happy or good within you, it will all come back to you multiplied ten thousand times. In the kingdom of love there is no competition; there is no possessiveness or control. The more love you give away, the more love you will have."*

-John O'Donohue
Anam Cara: A Book of Celtic Wisdom

The word karma comes from the Sanskrit language, which is the modern language of Hinduism and Jainism. Common translations include: "action," "effect," or "fate."

So, what is karma?

Karma is a difficult notion to conceptualize, particularly for cultures unfamiliar with the theory of reincarnation. With regard to karma being an action, or the sum of your actions... *it can be any action, or deed.*

Karma can even be something which we may dismiss as unimportant, or unexpressed, such as a thought.

And so, karma really is the sum total of every thought and every action we take in our life. *It all carries an effect, or consequences on the world around us.*

'Karmas' are classified into three types: *sanchita, prarabda, and agami:*

Sanchita karma is our *accumulated past actions*, which are waiting to come to fruition. It is the storehouse of every action we have ever made, in all the lifetimes we have ever lived... all of the *unresolved* past actions which are waiting to reach resolution.

Our **Prarabda karma** is the sum total of our *present actions*: what we are doing now, in this lifetime, and its *results which will be faced in this lifetime.*

Lord Krishna, the Hindu god of compassion, tenderness, and love, and worshipped as the 8th incarnation of the Hindu god Vishnu, said that *knowledge is the vehicle by which karma is burned or extinguished.*

The goal, in realizing the existence and importance of these two types of karma, through knowledge, is to understand and act accordingly, so that they may be extinguished in this lifetime. *They can then become guides for living a better life now, while clearing out our detrimental past, so that:*

Our **Agami karma,** stored from the actions of our present life, and waiting to present to us in the future *will only impact our next life in a positive way.*

Give us your thoughts on the concept of karma. Please describe in your own words how you interpret this concept, and the role that knowledge plays in your life, according to the teachings of Karma.

JOURNALING ASSIGNMENT 13.1

To get you started, give these thought-provoking questions some consideration:

- *Do I believe in karma?*
- *Do I believe in reincarnation?*
- *Does my awareness of this concept influence my behavior?*

_____

_____

_____

_____

_____

_____

_____

_____

_____

_____

CHAPTER 14

The Science of Meditation

SELF-DIRECTED NEUROPLASTICITY, MEDITATION AND THE BRAIN

The science of why all of these practices really work.

In his book, *The Mind & The Brain (Neuroplasticity and the Power of Mental Force),* researcher Dr. Jeffery Schwartz makes a compelling argument that you aren't at the mercy of genetically-predetermined brain activity. His research suggests that you play an active role in influencing brain function by deciding where to focus your attention.

What is neuroplasticity?

Neuroplasticity is a concept referring to the idea that the brain is capable of changing its function in response to your environment, thinking, emotions, and behavior. It was once thought that the brain was "fixed" in the way that it functioned after childhood.

That thinking evolved, and it was next conjectured that our teenage years were the final stage of brain development, but now, we know differently, and although it's likely that the brain is fully developed by our mid-20s, it is still capable of change. *Neuroplasticity refers to what we've discovered are ongoing changes we can make in neural pathways for life.*

What is self-directed neuroplasticity?

The brain remains neuroplastic for life. Self-directed neuroplasticity, as a practice, allows us to consciously control how we want our brains to work. It is our choice, and it is a matter of repetition. We see this at work when, at any age, we learn a new skill.

How Self-Directed Neuroplasticity Works

The theory of self-directed neuroplasticity takes this further, in suggesting that **the mind** is responsible for controlling **the brain**.

Although many remain skeptical, Schwartz makes a great argument for this, arguing that, if we don't have a mind, then we have no degree of self-control, and are therefore at the mercy of our brains. *Let that sink in for a moment.* The mind is something different than the brain.

FILL THE BRAIN WITH high thoughts, HIGHEST IDEALS, place them day and night before you, and out of that will come GREAT WORK.

— Swami Vivekananda

Most people would agree that it's just conveniently dismissive to say that we have no control over what we do. Even if you don't acknowledge that your mind controls your brain, it's hard to dismiss the physiology of it.

Our more evolved brain regions (such as our prefrontal cortex) are responsible, if we choose, for controlling our lower order, more primitive regions of the brain. This allows for the concept, and the practice of exerting self-control.

Making this informed kind of choice, the more that we make it… in turn changes our behavior, and the changes are rooted in the neuroplastic nature of our brain. In other words, yes… our mind is something different than our brain. *And that's a good thing!*

The concept of self-directed neuroplasticity involves:

Attention

Just about anything can catch our attention at any given moment in time. That's just the by-product of exposing your brain to various stimuli, while not being particularly present.

However, you *can* have full control over the amount of attention to which you give *anything*… whether it's an object, a thought, or a behavior.

It's your choice. You could have a depressing thought and give it a lot of attention (only serving to further magnify it), or you could choose to let it pass, and refocus on something else. The goal is to pay attention to what you want, so that your brain lights up and rewires to accommodate your desires.

Volition (willpower)

Simply paying attention is great, but attention alone won't really change anything. You need to actually get down in your own trenches and put in some work.

If you're trying to change your tendency towards acting impulsively, first of all, congratulations. Beyond that, you need a plan to refocus your attention, and the actions you take habitually, so that you can begin to change the way your brain is firing.

With consistent practice, your brain will begin to fire up the circuits associated with the new behavior, rather than the unwanted one. *Practice is essential.*

Brain activation

This is why practice is important here. The regions of the brain which begin to activate through practice do so because of repetition. For instance, focusing on happiness is an entirely different matter to your brain's physiology than being chronically depressed. Remember, you are mapping impressions of *everything* to your brain. The more impressions you lay down, the more predominant and accessible those outcomes will be.

Consistency ("If You Don't Use It, You Lose It")

Regions within your brain are constantly in competition for prioritizing the way in which they carrying out various, and often unrelated functions.

Whichever regions you use more often will effectively overpower the other regions and get more neural (consciousness) real-estate. The regions and neural pathways that you use less frequently will get less real-estate, may become compromised, and possibly, eventually shut down.

This is why we need to take an inventory of our daily habits so that we can be more mindful of what they do to our conscious awareness, to our ability to communicate with ourselves, and with others.

Here's a few brain facts

Size:

The brain is about 3 pounds of tofu-like tissue, comprised of over a hundred billion brain cells.

Activity:

The brain is *always* on, 24/7, providing us instant, on-demand access to information. This is one of our body's most protected organs, encased in the skull, receiving between 20 - 25% of the body's blood flow and oxygen supply, and as much as 50% of our glucose.

The importance of blood and oxygen is obvious. But why glucose? *Because it's fuel.* Glucose is the most important sugar in our bodies, and also the primary source of fuel for our brains.

The brain is our most energy-demanding organ, and how well we think, learn, and remember are a function of our glucose levels, and how efficiently our brains use it as a fuel source.

Speed:
The neurons in the brain are specialized cells that transmit, receive, and process information. On average, neurons fire off messages at the rate of about 200 times a second and each one connects with about a thousand other neurons. So, each time a neuron sends a message, about 1,000 others receive that information.

There is always conversation about what wins… our brains, or a computer. The jury is still out as far as speed is concerned. But in its efficient use of energy, *the brain wins hands down.*

There is a lot going on in our brains. In fact, by most counts, *we are not conscious of ninety-five percent of it.* The five percent of brain activity of which we *are* consciously aware consists of the choices we make: decisions, our emotional state, the actions we take, and the behaviors we choose in social interactions.

The brain is the headquarters of our nervous system. *But the brain is not the mind, and the mind is not the brain.*

Even though a lot of the brain's real estate lives in a unconscious state, the brain is still the headquarters of our nervous system, and the nervous system represents information. **How that information flows, how it is directed—some call the mind.**

And yet, *the mind is what the brain does,* and the brain depends on the nervous system, which intertwines with and depends on other bodily systems, which interface with, intertwine with, and are often co-dependent upon completely external factors, such as social and cultural norms.

Reciprocally, the brain can be what the mind tells it to be. *It is quite the dance.*

The brain can change the mind... *for better, and for worse.* For example:

For the better:

A little caffeine can improve our thinking, and our alertness.

For the worse:

Too much alcohol can cause imbalances in our neurotransmitters, lessening our ability to accurately and reliably process information.

And the mind can change the brain, often in ways of which we are completely unaware.

Thoughts which are of no consequence, immaterial, map to neural activity in the brain, which *is* material. It is material because, impression after impression, these thoughts of no matter become more and more worn in as "wired" pathways.

Our neurons begin to more and more easily synchronize these patterns through repetition, and our body increases the supply of oxygen and glucose to building, maintaining and strengthening them.

The axiom is:

"Neurons that fire together, wire together."

We also know this by another word: *habit.*

This all serves to underline the importance of consistent mindfulness practices. *It can rewire your brain, both in the moment, and in more enduring ways that become woven into the fabric of your consciousness.*

This is using your mind to change your brain to change your mind for the better. *This is at the core of the concept of self-directed neuroplasticity.*

The research emphatically supports it. *Let's look at some of the neuroplastic things that begin to happen as an outcome of the practice of* **meditation***:*

Physiological

- Thickens the prefrontal regions of the brain (that help control attention)
- Thickens the insula (supporting our self-awareness and empathy)
- Increases gray matter density (supporting memory function)
- Inhibits the amygdala from over-reaction (regulating fight-or-flight responses)
- Increases activation of left frontal brain regions (lifting mood)
- Increases overall brain connectivity (improving awareness in the moment)

Psychological

- Improves focus and attention (including attention deficit disorders)
- Increases compassion Increases empathy Reduces insomnia, anxiety, phobias, and eating disorders

At the highest level, self-directed neuroplasticity, whether it is accommodated by meditation, or by any of the other mindfulness practices we've mentioned can support a sea-change in our world view... a difference between "doing" and "being." These dual modes of perception are polar, but at the highest level describe us all.

Some of the characteristics of these two ways in which we look out at the world include:

Doing	Being
Constant verbal activity	Little verbal activity
Past-focused	Now-focused
Goal-directed	In the moment
Craving	Contented
Focal, myopic view	Panoramic view
Judgmental / Evaluative	Non-judgmental
Wandering mind	Mindful presence

We may be some mix of these characteristics, *as we are all works in progress*. But it's important to spend some time with each of them, which we'd encourage you to do now.

JOURNALING ASSIGNMENT 14.1

Pick one pair of characteristics now, and tell us where you believe you fit in, and how you feel about it. If that characteristic falls within the "doing" category, in what do you believe that behavior is rooted?

For example, if you are goal-directed, what is it about the present you that is less than what you believe the future you will be? Are you uncomfortable living in the moment with the present you? Why? If so, does that make you see the world from a position of lack? Is that fair to you, and others in your life?

_____

_____

_____

_____

_____

_____

_____

_____

_____

_____

_____

_____

_____

_____

_____

_____

_____

_____

_____

The brain is still one of the most powerful tools that you may ever have at your disposal. In large part, what it can do, and what you can do with it is really *your call.* **Thoughts become things.** Why not use *your thoughts to condition your brain to do the best things it (you) possibly can?*

CHAPTER 15

Our Sacred Alignments

Even after all this time,
the sun never says to the earth
'YOU OWE ME.'
Look what happens with
a love like that.
It lights the whole sky.

- Hafez

HONORING MOTHER EARTH
Recognizing and respecting the miracle on which we live.

"Let us think of Mother Earth."

–Native American prayer

We live on a miracle. And yet many have chosen to forget that it is life itself. All of it. And as we weep for what we more easily see as our fellow living beings here who struggle to survive… the rest of this Earth is no different.

We politicize, we marginalize, and we minimize the pain that Mother Earth, Gaia, is in. That she is not suffering from climate change, or the garbage that we litter everywhere. That our entire eco-balance is failing, and that we are losing entire species of life daily due to our greed, our politics, and our lack of respect.

But she is life itself. Every square inch of her. Life in which the same stardust is shared, only expressed in a different way than we are. That makes it no less. We once understood this and embraced the unity of all living things. Perhaps we have come to deny it in what we would like to believe is our educated ascendancy. That we are conscious beings, and all of the rest which doesn't speak our language must be something less.

But this is not winning. This is not even surviving. It is a duality that has no place in our world. Because as surely as every light casts a shadow, we are a part of, not distinct from—this complex world on which we live. There is a sacred interdependence here. The ancients knew this. Spiritual masters and contemplatives still do:

"All things connect. Man did not weave the
web of life, he is merely a strand in it.
Whatever he does to the web,
he does to himself."

–Chief Seattle

And so, if you find yourself disconnected from this truth, we encourage you to remember. That this connection is not only real, but it is of vital importance to all dimensions of our health. Without it, every living thing will eventually stress from the dis-ease of separation.

Do some soul-searching with Mother Earth in mind.

Think about why we would choose that name for this planet on which we live. The hospitality with which she shows us so much life in the midst of the cold, dark space that surrounds us. The food that she provides us. The resonance that her nights and days creates within each of us. The rhythm of night turning to day.

Do you take time, and pause to reflect on that miracle? To express your gratitude, your humility that this is home? That her gravity keeps us physically grounded, that her atmosphere allows our lungs to fill with air, as her greenery nourishes us, day in and day out? *It is remarkable.* Nothing is as Sacred as this Mother is to us all. She needs your love.

JOURNALING ASSIGNMENT 15.1

So, what's your relationship to Mother Earth? If you've never spent any time considering that, now's your opportunity, and here's *some questions you can ask yourself to get the ball rolling.*

How do you currently treat Mother Earth? Do you believe that you have a symbiotic relationship with her, or do you see the Earth as just a planet with resources that you can use?

_____

_____

_____

_____

_____

Being connected to nature is an important aspect of your spiritual health, and of establishing and maintaining your connection to the Earth. That can take many forms... gardening, hiking, surfing, camping, walking, and much more. How do you currently connect to nature? How does it make you feel? If you don't, what might you try?

_____

_____

_____

_____

_____

_____

How can you enhance your relationship with our planet? What can you do to help protect her?

_____

_____

_____

_____

_____

_____

Tell us about two different places in nature that you find beautiful. Make sure that one location is near where you live *(we sometimes take these for granted)*.

Name of 1ˢᵗ Place _____

What do you see *(what catches your eye about this place)*?

_____

_____

_____

_____

_____

What does it remind you of *(how do you relate to this place)***? How does it make you feel?**

_____

_____

_____

_____

_____

Name of 2nd Place _____

What do you see *(what catches your eye about this place)***?**

_____

_____

_____

_____

_____

What does it remind you of *(how do you relate to this place)***? How does it make you feel?**

_____

_____

_____

_____

_____

Tell us how you felt about this process of mindfully exploring nature.
Was it different from the way you usually look at nature? How?

_____

_____

_____

_____

_____

The new physics provides a modern version of ancient spirituality.

In a universe made out of energy, everything is one.

- Bruce Lipton

GETTING TO THE HEART OF THE MATTER
Spirituality arises from the heart.

It should come as no surprise that it's our belief that spirituality arises from the heart. It is a very unique, loving, and creative space in which to live. When you are there, you know you are there. But stressors in our lives can often leave us living from our head space, and not our heart space, and often, not even notice. *So, it's important to recognize where we're coming from as we look out onto our world.*

This is especially true in the beginnings of our travels. When we start out, taking our first steps on the path towards our own, unique and living spirituality, we are often oblivious to our real voice. *Our authentic self.*

It is only in the process of our self-assessment that we begin to understand what is authentic about our voice, and what is inherited, often from those who we admire and for whom we believe with the greatest respect.

When we begin to seek out the real origins of our world view, *we begin to understand intuitively what is ours, and what is not.* What limits our view of ourselves, and our potential for ourselves. What makes us judgmental, of ourselves, and of others.

It is important, then, to have some reliable tools with which to do a self-check every now and then, and ask the question: "What space am I living in? My head, or my heart?" *We all need this very special kind of scheduled maintenance no matter what age, no matter what our experience or consistency of spiritual practice.*

Are you living in your head, rather than your heart? While it affects everyone around you, you really need look no further than yourself, ask a few very simple questions, and commit to an honest response:

Am I being kind to myself?
Would anyone want to be spoken to in the way that I'm speaking to myself?
Am I supportive of who I am?
Am I loving to myself?
Do I support myself, unconditionally?

If the answer to one or more of these questions is "no," then you are in your head, rationalizing your behavior, and failing to empower who you really are. Your mind chatter has taken you from the present moment, and in some cases, all the way back to your childhood conditioning, including your inherited responses to personal challenges.

This often means that others, not you are the ones who are determining who you are. As their view of you changes, so does yours. *That's simply not authentic.*

Are you living in your heart, rather than your head? Again, look in the mirror, ask a few very simple questions, and commit to an honest response:

- *Do I feel aligned with who I am?*
- *Am I guided by my personal feelings, or those of others?*
- *Do I feel free of undue anxiety?*
- *Do I like myself… who I am, and what I stand for?*
- *Am I open to personal growth?*
- *Have I stopped self-critically judging myself?*

If the answers here are "yes," then you are back on the path to your greatest good. You are empowered to be self-compassionate. You are able to heal. And you are able to celebrate and honor yourself.

Congratulations. You're on a mindful path towards ***living your spirituality***.

SUGGESTED READINGS ON SPIRITUALITY

Here's a short list of some of our favorite books. They've offered us untold support and ongoing insight in our travels along our spiritual paths. We hope that you'll enjoy and benefit from them as we have. If you have personal favorites as well, we'd love to hear from you!

Le Petit Prince, *Antoine de Saint-Exupéry*

On the Brink of Everything, *Parker Palmer*

The Power of Now, *Eckhart Tolle*

Brave New Earth, *Eckhart Tolle*

The Celestine Prophecy, *James Redfield*

The Alchemist, *Paulo Coelho*

The Four Agreements, *Paulo Coelho*

The Untethered Soul (The journey beyond yourself), *Michael Singer*

The Knowing Heart, *Kabir Helminski*

The Wisdom Way of Knowing, *Cynthia Bourgeault*

Wisdom Jesus, *Cynthia Bourgeault*

The Prophet, *Kahlil Gibran*

The Miracle of Mindfulness, *Thich Nhat Hanh*

Trusting God, *Jerry Bridges*

The Sacred Art of Loving-Kindness, *Rami Shapiro*

Interspiritual Meditation, *Ed Bastian*

Autobiography of a Yogi, *Paramahansa Yogananda*

In an emergency

A few resources available to you in times of crisis.

Worried about a friend? Dealing with some issues of your own?

There are trained people who can help. And if you're in immediate danger, please call 911 or your local police station.

General Crisis Support by Text
  Crisis Text Line
  Text **SUPPORT** to 741-741 (24/7)

Depression and Suicide
  National Suicide Prevention Hotline
  (800) 273-8255

  The Trevor Project - Saving LBTGQ Lives
  (866) 488-7386

Dating Abuse and Domestic Violence
  National Domestic Violence Hotline
  (800) 799-7233

  RAINN: Rape, Abuse, and Incest National Network
  (800) 656 4673

Child Abuse
  Childhelp National Child Abuse Hotline
  (800) 422-4453

  National Safe Place - Runaways, Homeless, and At-Risk Youth
  Text **SAFE** and your current location to the number 69866

  National Runaway Safeline
  (800) 786-2929

Poison Control
  American Association of Poison Control Centers
  (800) 222-1222

Journal Assignment Index

Chapter 1
1.1; 10
1.2; 12

Chapter 2
2.1; 15

Chapter 3
3.1; 35
3.2; 44
3.3; 50
3.4; 52
3.5; 63
3.6; 70

Chapter 4
4.1; 75
4.2; 84

Chapter 5
5.1; 90

Chapter 6
6.1; 104
6.2; 108
6.3; 110

Chapter 7
7.1; 115
7.2; 118

Chapter 8
8.1; 123
8.2; 128
8.3; 131

Chapter 9
9.1; 140
9.2; 142

Chapter 10
10.1, 157
10.2; 159
10.3; 162

Chapter 11
11.1; 169
11.2; 171
11.3; 174
11.4; 177
11.5; 183

Chapter 12
12.1; 193
12.2; 195
12.3; 201
12.4; 205
12.5; 213
12.6; 223
12.7; 225
12.8; 230

Chapter 13
13.1; 236

Chapter 14
14.1; 246

Chapter 15
15.1; 250

INDEX

Abraham(ic), 34, 81

acceptance, 14, 19, 27, 52, 63, 96, 104, 154–155, 158, 181, 188

affirming, 158, 210

Allah, 19, 211
    See also Islam

allowing, 4, 144–145, 196, 221

American, 2, 16, 80, 172, 186, 204, 214, 249

amygdala, 123, 245

Anam Cara: A Book of Celtic Wisdom (O'Donohue, John), 235

anger, 14, 25, 49, 54, 86, 96, 102, 122, 159, 182, 187, 206, 229

appreciation, 37, 52, 70, 158, 194

Aristotle, 139

attention, 1, 29, 41, 50, 58–59, 80, 92, 109, 117, 119–120, 127, 135, 137, 139, 141–142, 144, 149–150, 154, 157, 163, 168, 173–174, 179, 188, 196–197, 221, 239, 241, 245

attitude, 11–12, 20, 26, 98, 114, 130, 153, 169, 224

Australia, 17

Adventures of Huckleberry Finn (Twain, Mark), 118

awareness, 14–15, 19–22, 26, 38, 50, 63, 87, 92, 99, 108–109, 125, 127, 136–138, 143, 146, 149–150, 157, 164, 168, 170, 173, 178, 197, 206, 209, 217–218, 221, 236, 242, 245

Baha'i Temple, 81

Bahá'u'lláh, 81

balancing, 20, 23, 218, 222

bargaining, 187–188

Bastian, Ed, 80

beauty, 37, 75, 89, 93, 99

beginner's mind, 103, 153–154, 202

behaviors, 11, 20–22, 109–110, 152, 176, 217, 243

being, 9–10, 32–33, 49, 75, 92, 117, 128, 149, 210, 245

beliefs, 9, 11–12, 19–20, 26–27, 29, 55, 67, 69–70, 74, 82, 130, 207, 219, 254

Bhagavad Gita, the, 189

Black Elk, 151

Bloomberg Ranking–World's Healthiest Countries, 16

body, 7, 16, 32–33, 49–50, 52, 80, 123, 137, 139, 143, 145–147, 153, 165, 190, 198, 207, 213, 217–218, 221, 229–231, 242, 244

Borysenko, Joan, 80

Bourgeault, Cynthia, 80

brain activation, 242

breath, 31, 34, 50, 136, 138–139, 145–146, 156, 173, 190

Brother Wayne Teasdale, 79

Buddha, 19, 26, 39, 78, 81, 134–136, 198, 228–229
    Buddha Mind, 9, 33, 78

Buddha's Brain: The Practical Neuroscience of Happiness, Love and Wisdom (Hanson, Rick), 149

carbon footprint. *See* Environmental Wellness

caring, 37, 61, 93

Chakra, 206, 217 *(illustration),* 218–223
    Crown, 218, 221
    Heart, 206–207, 219–220
    Root, 206, 218–219, 221
    Sacral, 219
    Solar-Plexus, 219
    Third Eye, 220
    Throat, 206, 220
chants, 135, 172,
    See also mantras
Chardin, Pierre Teilhard de, 4, 126, 179
Chief Seattle, 249
Chopra, Deepak, 18, 32
Christ, 33, 82
    Christ Consciousness, 9, 19
    Christian(ity), 34, 79–80, 135–136, 196, 202, 212, 214
communication, 21–22, 29, 47, 49, 55, 62–63, 131, 181, 206, 218, 220, 222
    communicator, 22
compassion, 1, 3, 14, 19, 37, 54–55, 63, 67, 94, 100, 104, 124–125, 168–169, 172–173, 176, 178, 208, 212, 220, 229, 231, 236, 245, 255
conflict, 22, 141
Confucious, 135
connection, 7, 9, 29, 31, 41, 50, 56, 71, 79–80, 86–87, 89, 92, 94, 132, 170, 181, 183, 186, 188, 198, 206, 208, 213, 221–222, 250–251
consistency, 63, 210, 242, 254
contemplatio, 196, 203

Dalai Lama, 1, 137, 167, 192
Dass, Ram, 37

denial, 154, 187
depression, 54, 93, 122, 144, 188, 206, 211, 225
Desiderata (Ehrmann, Max), 198–200
devotion, 26, 43, 63, 94
Dickens, Charles, 74
dignity, 94, 98
dimension(s), 7, 9, 15–17, 19, 20–22, 29, 65, 77, 80, 92, 95, 98, 104, 128, 130–131, 144, 149, 152, 176, 181, 205, 250
    dimensional, 17, 19, 225
    dimensionality, 17
Divine, 4–5, 9, 33, 40, 52, 74, 77, 80–81, 86, 94, 98, 130, 172, 195, 202, 208, 217, 221, 223
dogma, 27–28, 34, 98, 101, 103, 141, 210
    dogmatic, 14, 27
doing, 117, 245–246
dream(s), 7, 38, 70, 96, 190, 200
drugs, 20–21, 186
duality, 25–26, 75, 101, 249
Dyer, Wayne, 33, 234

ego, 4, 7, 26, 38, 40, 54, 96, 130, 137, 150, 154, 168, 181, 206
Ekaku, Hakuin, 142
Emotional Wellness, 20
empathy, 3, 19, 54, 63, 95, 101, 125, 245
enthusiasm, 63, 95
Environmental Wellness, 21
equanimity, 1, 19, 95, 124–125, 127
Erlandson, Sven, 2
Euripides, 199
exemplar, 77, 81, 83–84
expectation, 98, 100, 122–123

faith, 1, 54, 79–81, 83, 95, 99, 101, 183, 221

family(ies), 2, 36, 41–42, 56, 63, 67, 70, 78, 87, 93–94, 109, 141, 173, 175, 179, 193–195

Father Thomas Keating, 80, 196

Ford, Debbie, 32

Forgive(ness), 14, 19, 52, 56, 59, 86, 96, 141, 159, 220, 224, 228–232

Four Immeasurables, the, 124–125

Fox, Matthew, 4

Franklin, DeVon, 32

Friend(ships), 22, 36, 41–43, 56, 62–63, 67, 70, 78–79, 82, 94, 109, 111, 141, 173, 175, 179, 194, 195, 209

fulfillment, 19, 21, 181

    See also meaning; purpose

Full Catastrophe Living, (Kabat-Zinn, Jon), 152, 164

    See also Kabat-Zinn, Jon

Gaia. *See* Mother Earth

Gaytaso, Tenzin. *See* Dalai Lama

Germany, 17, 185

God, 9, 19, 25–26, 32–34, 42, 52, 70, 78–81, 136, 187, 189–190, 195–196, 200, 202, 204, 210–211, 221, 236

grace, 38, 56, 63, 67, 79, 96, 99, 114, 139, 156, 187, 200

gratitude, 41, 63, 93, 96, 99, 104, 114–115, 158, 163, 172, 224–225, 250

    gratitude quotient, GQ, 225

Great Spirit, 9, 212

Greater Good Science Center, the, 225

Ground of Being, The, 9, 210

Hafez, 248

Hahn, Thich Nhat, 36, 78, 161

Halvorson, Heidi Grant. *See* Motivation Science Center

Harvey, Andrew, 4

Health & the Human Spirit (Seaward, Brian Luke), 131–132

HeartMath Institute, 47

Helminski, Camille and Kabir, 80

Hero's Journey, 7

higher purpose, 5, 181

Hindu, Hinduism, 34, 130, 135–136, 140, 143, 207, 211–212, 217, 235–236

holistic, 3, 89, 144, 152, 207, 229

honesty, 40, 63, 96, 98, 131, 156, 173, 177–178, 181, 229

hope, 7, 54, 74, 96, 99, 137, 190, 197

hospitality, 98, 110, 250

Houston, Jean, 33, 80

humility, 19, 54, 63, 77, 98, 100, 207, 250

imagination, 63, 98, 177, 217, 220

integrity, 1, 3, 63, 98, 168, 179, 183

Intellectual Wellness, 20

interconnectedness, 14, 34, 129, 183

intuition, 9, 59, 130, 142, 154, 220

IONS Conscious Aging program, 56

Islam, 34, 135–136, 211

    See also Allah

Israel, 17

It Was A Very Good Year (Drake, Ervin), 129

Italy, 17, 79

Jainism. *See* Hinduism

Jalaledin Rumi, 80, 180

Japan, 17, 141, 153

Jehovah, 19

  See also Yahweh

Jesus, of Nazareth, 26, 78, 81, 198

  See also Christ

Jobs, Steve, 82

joy, 44, 49, 54, 99, 101, 115, 172, 190, 219, 225

  sympathetic, 125

Judaism, 34, 82, 101, 135–136

Jung, Carl, 38, 175–176, 214

  See also ego

justice, 59, 99

Kabat-Zinn, Jon, 1, 143, 149, 152, 164

karma, 206, 235–236

  Agami, 235–236

  Prarabda, 235

  Sanchita, 235

Keller, Helen, 199

kindness, 3, 14, 19, 54, 63, 99, 110, 124, 140–141,

  152, 172–173, 182, 193–195, 221

koan, 141–142

Krishna, 81, 236

Lakota Sioux, 212

Lectio Divina, 195–196, 198, 201–202

letting go, 96, 155

Lipton, Bruce, 253

listening, 40, 62, 70, 99, 109, 125, 168–173

love, 5, 29, 33, 37, 41, 49, 52, 54, 56, 61, 63, 70,

  78–79, 86, 92–93, 95, 99–100, 104, 110, 124,

love (*cont.*), 136, 140–141, 155–156, 182, 196,

  198, 200, 219–220, 222, 235–236, 250

McClain, Constance, CM, 19, 36, 66, 77, 97,

  185, 204

mandala, 214–215, 216 *(illustration)*

mantra(s), 83, 135, 143, 210–213

meaning, 4, 7, 15, 19, 29, 31, 42, 55, 65, 100–101,

  130, 168, 205

  See also fulfillment; purpose

meditatio, 196, 202

meditation(s), 14, 62, 87, 89, 124, 135–144, 147,

  152, 154, 170, 195, 208–209, 212, 214, 220,

  223, 239, 244–245

Mental Wellness, 20

metaphysically, 7

Metta, 124, 140–141

Meyers-Briggs, 58, 61

modalities, 25

Moses, 81–82

Mother Earth, 2, 130, 152, 222, 249–250

Mother Teresa, 79, 82, 227

Motivation Science Center, 120

mudra, 206–209

  Abhaya, 209 *(illustration)*

  Anjali or Namaste, 206–208 *(illustration)*

  Jnana or Gyan, 208 *(illustration)*

  Pala, 209 *(illustration)*

  Prana, 209 *(illustration)*

Muhammed, 48, 81

Netherlands, 17

non-duality, 25–26, 125

non-judgment(ally), 2–3, 11, 95, 100, 125, 143, 149–150, 153, 178, 207, 245
    non-judging, 152
non-striving, 154
nurturing, 75, 100
nutritional, 21

Occupational Wellness, 21
Om, *(illustration)* 212
On Death (Gibran, Kahlil), 190
On Death and Dying (Kübler-Ross, Elisabeth), 186
openness, 101
oratio, 196, 203

patience, 19, 63, 99, 109, 153–154
patterns, 22, 103, 122, 145, 162, 176, 214–215, 217, 219, 220, 244
peace, 20, 34, 49, 54–55, 63, 79, 86–87, 89, 101, 110, 124, 127, 141, 153, 199–200, 209–210, 219, 221, 228
Pelletier, Dr. Kenneth R., 16
Pew Research Center, The, 2, 34
Phillips, Jan, 52
Physical Wellness, 21
physiological, 144, 210, 222, 245
psychological(ly), 7, 101, 135, 144, 217, 222, 245
Pink, Daniel, 32
play, 101, 103
presence, 31, 33, 52, 104, 108–109, 120, 125, 127, 137, 156, 168, 170, 198, 207, 221–222, 245
present, be, 28, 36, 56, 93, 117, 120, 122, 135, 139, 164

purpose, 4–5, 7, 15, 19, 29, 32, 55, 63, 81, 83, 100, 130, 139, 157–158
    See also fulfillment; meaning

quest, questing, 101–102, 104, 135, 150

Rahman, A.R., 8
religions, 2, 14, 26–29, 31–32, 35, 81, 211–212
Resurfacing: Techniques for Exploring Consciousness (Palmer, Harry), 175
reverence, 3, 15, 63, 86, 102, 152, 168, 181
rumination, 122

sacred activism, 4
Sagan, Carl, 68
Saint Francis of Assisi, 79
Sandbach, John, 204
Satan, 25
SBNR, 2, 34
Spirituality and Health (Seaward, Brian Luke), 80
self-assessment, 15, 20, 25, 81, 131, 169, 254
shadow, 14, 28, 42, 102, 175–178, 249
silence, 102, 138, 171–172, 190, 199, 214
Singapore, 17
Singer, Michael, 33
Social Wellness, 22
soul, 3, 31–35, 77, 129–130, 156, 183, 199–200, 206, 250
Source, 9, 19, 42, 70, 81, 86, 211, 221
Spain, 17
Spiritual Wellness, 19

spirit, 7–8, 16–17, 32, 34, 37, 42, 52, 60, 63, 86, 89, 98, 100, 102–104, 132, 142, 144, 153, 156, 181, 189–190, 196–197, 199–200, 202–203, 205, 207, 212, 223

Spiritual Health, 3, 14–15, 20, 47, 51, 53, 61–62, 72, 80, 93, 98, 131, 135–136, 209, 251

spiritual transformation, 7, 9–10, 92

Stowe, Harriet Beecher, 228

Sweden, 17

Switzerland, 17, 185

symptoms, 3, 16–17, 146, 211

Tao Te Ching, Taoists, 19, 23, 74, 135, 214

The Hero's Journey: Joseph Campbell on His Life & Work (Campbell, Joseph), 7

The Mind & The Brain (Neuroplasticity and the Power of Mental Force) (Schwartz, Dr. Jeffery), 239

Thoreau, Henry David, 56

Tolle, Eckhart, 33, 107

traditions, 1, 70–71, 135, 143, 150, 207, 214

trust, 38, 40, 49, 90, 130–131, 154, 182–183, 190, 209

Tyson, Neil deGrasse, 88

Tzu, Lao, 23, 26, 74–75, 135, 199
See also Tao Te Ching

United States, U.S., 1, 16

unity, 27–28, 75, 95, 98, 100–101, 103–104, 221, 249

Value(s), 4, 15, 27–28, 55–56, 58–59, 62–65, 67, 71, 83, 96, 108, 130, 160, 176, 181, 186

Vanzant, Iyanla, 32

Vaughan-Lee, Llewellyn, 33

Visio Divina, 202

vision, 2, 5, 38, 40, 44, 63, 69, 72, 81, 103, 199

Vivekananda, Swami, 240

volition, 241

Walker, James Anthony, JW, 22, 81, 205

Wallace, Alan. *See* Four Immeasurables, the

Weinberg, Rabbi Noah, 57

Williamson, Marianne, 33

Wolves, Two, 54

wonder, 5, 15, 27, 34, 93, 101–103

Woodman, Marion, 184

X - factor, the, 103

Yahweh, 19
See also Jehovah

yearning, 2, 104, 157

yoga, 89, 124, 143, 145, 206, 209, 213

zeal, 104

zest, 104

Zoma, Ben, 76

Zukav, Gary, 32

Zoroaster, 81

CONSTANCE McCLAIN
BIO

Reverend Constance McClain is a lifelong spiritual seeker. Along that path, she became a spiritual mentor through the Claritas Institute of Spiritual Mentoring & Inquiry, a program designed and brought to life by Joan Borysenko. Furthering her dream of becoming a minister, she is a graduate of The Spiritual Paths Institute of InterSpirituality in Santa Barbara, California.

Her love of dance, hiking and helping others prompted her to become certified as a Master Exercise Specialist through the Cooper Institute in Dallas, TX, where she then pursued a career in Somatic Education with a primary focus on integrated movement… designed to guide students and clients into an embodied awareness of the Inner Spirit within.

A completely unexpected near death experience in 2013, which continues to leave her left side largely paralyzed brought her an increased sense of urgency to become more deeply in service… and in 2017, her enduring dream of ministry was fulfilled, and she was ordained as an InterFaith/InterSpiritual minister through the One Spirit Interfaith Seminary.

Today, Constance has an unwaivering perspective: that her love of life, all things sacred, holy and divine continue to support her through even the most life-changing of adversities, and it is being mindful of this spiritual dimension of health that is at the very core of *Mindful Paths: Steps Towards a Living Spirituality*.

JAMES ANTHONY WALKER
BIO

Reverend James Anthony Walker began his formal studies in music composition at Boston University, and later as a Graduate Teaching Fellow and founding Director of the Computer Music Studio at The University of Chicago. While today much of his work is best described as 'painting with sound,' he still finds it a distinct honor to have studied with a number of Pulitzer Prize winners, as well as many gifted mentors along the way.

He was ordained in 2017 by the One Spirit Interfaith Ministry, and today he blends his musical vision, his years of research into generative techniques, and his spirituality… into transformative ambient music that has been highly acclaimed for use with meditation, relaxation, therapy for the sleep-deprived, and supportive environments for a wide variety of somatic practices.

Today, he and life partner Rev. Constance McClain co-direct Oasis of the Heart, an inclusive InterFaith/InterSpiritual ministry without walls… drawing spiritual nourishment from the core tenets of many of the world's great wisdom paths, and together, they seek to promote a deeper understanding of the beliefs we all share in common, so that we can begin to better embrace our differences.

It has been his joy to collaborate on this book, as he has been witness to the life-changing effects that this work, through Constance's mentorship, has brought to so many over the years.